THROWAWAY

Throwaway

Barry Harden

The events and conversations in this book have been set down
to the best of the author's ability, although some names have been
changed to protect the privacy of individuals.

First paperback edition February 2025

ISBN 979-8-9923708-0-5 (paperback)
ISBN 979-8-9923708-1-2 (e-Book)

www.barryhardenauthor.com

Introduction

I was fed and I was watered and, in a fashion, cared for, but most of the time, I was left to my own devices from a very young age, as were many of my generation. As a result, odd things happened and the path that I trod, though full of adventure, inevitably led nowhere. Having reached that negative position, I was able to observe, marvel at, and participate in many things that a person with a modicum of focus or brains might have missed. I have tried to make this memoir an amusing account of someone who was never quite able to climb over the fence and who often fell face first into the mud.

Throwaway is set mostly in the NW suburbs of London and details my personal recollections from about 1950 to 1970. I am not going to pretend that this little history is a complete record of my observations and participation during the first decades after the Second World War. It is, however, a record of some of the things that shaped, or more precisely, pummelled me into what I am today, that is to say, surprised to still be here.

I started my career as a human child, painfully thin, and even now, I have been described as a 'racing snake', whatever that is, and I was always an embarrassment to my mother. As a result of this, she hated to be seen out with me. Neighbours and people in the street would remark, 'You should take him to the doctor. You might, though, have to have him put down. He'll not last the winter!' Dogs would snarl and bare their teeth as I passed, and horses would drag their carts and floats across the pavement to bar my way. I have been chased from a neighbour's kitchen for eating their dog's biscuits from a hessian sack and pelted with acorns by angry squirrels. It was as if I had been raised by a pack of wolves, and I pondered...was that the problem?

Personal histories are always difficult. Viewpoints change, people change, and history often changed to suit a situation. For me, recounting my history does not present a viewpoint problem as it does a chronological one. Events tend to overlap or collide or crop up again years later. So the best I can do is relate my adventures and observations in groups not constrained by time but by their relationship to each other.

Barry Harden
December 2023

1

It was around the end of January 1944 when my father said to my mother, 'Joan, bearing in mind that it's your birthday, and I did buy you a bag of sherbet lemons, I think we should copulate.'

They did, and I was the unfortunate item they produced. He obviously had a climax, she didn't, saying in later days that in all her ninety-two years, she had never had an orgasm. To add to the embarrassment, she announced this in a restaurant in a loud voice. It was at once followed by silence from all the other diners.

However, it was wartime, and not all things were expected to be rosy. Nor were they. The next nine months, two weeks and five days were not what she expected.

At the time, my mother was living with my four-year-old brother at my paternal grandparents' house in Lavenham, Suffolk, her own father living nearby at Long Mulford.

Having turned down the advances of my grandfather, she overheard him demand of my brother, 'Where is that whore, your mother?' He likely felt justified in his own mind being the sort of person that he was.

She recounted that on one occasion, he had caught his

fly buttons in her hair, not that it was any of her doing. It was the sort of thing that the swine would do to provoke her, like shoving his trouser front in her face when she was cleaning the floor. But it was only to be expected. That was who he was.

My father's mother played little or no part in this reality, but she was at one time her own person with an income, a property, and a one-year-old child. That would have been around 1915.

To make her living, my grandmother had taken in lodgers, probably forming a relationship with one and duly giving birth to my uncle, Stan. Her lover went to war and never returned like so many others, but the rumour was that the real father of the child was the butcher who lived just down the road. My grandfather, another of her lodgers, saw his chance on his predecessor's demise, and persuaded or coerced her to marry him. One must realise the pressure from society at that time and understand that her options were very limited.

Anyway, he got his own way and his evil intent had succeeded, and so this itinerant railway worker became, at one stroke, the master of the household, an expectant father and the tyrant who expelled his wife's young child from her house.

So it was no surprise that when I was born three weeks late, he decided it was not going to be there, and he expelled my mother also. Her own father was hardly sympathetic to her plight and sent her on her way as well, his second wife having just run off with a Black American serviceman.

It was only through the kindness of a friend who called a taxi that my mother arrived in the nick of time in Sudbury, Suffolk, at the old workhouse turned geriatric home, Walnut Tree Cottage Hospital. And there it happened—the midwife removed the cork and I arrived, a howling, overweight piglet at ten pounds four ounces, a hairy thing which a few minutes later turned into me with the help, of course, of lashings of obligatory boiling water and towels and a jolly good slap on the buttocks delivered, not to get me to breathe, but more likely to shut me up.

Whereas most people expecting a baby have some notion as to what to call that child, boy or girl, my mother's shock at the sight of me—'Oh, my god, he's as black as a blackberry!'— led to me being cursed with the name Barry. Blackberry would have suited me better, but in 1944, that would have probably been unacceptable.

In Lavenham, she would have been suspected of witchcraft and given a thoroughly good ducking in the local stream. Not only that, but the Irish midwife in attendance egged her on with 'Michael' and, in raptures, declared that they were both Irish names. What is not fair is that I wasn't really black at all; it was just that I was wet, sticky and had a mass of black hair.

The truth is that I would have been quite happy just to be called Berry, but it was not to be. At least I wouldn't have had to answer that pathetic question, 'Is Barry short for Barold?' No, it bloody well wasn't, and stop calling me Bow or Baz, the latter short for another horrendous name, Basil.

It is probably worth mentioning that my brother was

most distressed. He had already chosen my name, Jacqueline Stanley. Now that could have been interesting, possibly a life-changing experience.

2

Up to this moment, all of this is just related history, and little else of interest happened until I developed my first vestige of memory. It is difficult to put a date on my first recollection, but I would say that I was out of nappies, could walk, and was able to manipulate the catches on the side of my cot. I recall that I had regular times for activities—one was an afternoon nap, and another was an afternoon poo. These two things were closely linked, and so, when I awoke from my nap, I obviously had it in my mind to poo. It was simple or should have been.

It was a comfortably warm day, and I felt content when I awoke from my nap. As usual, the lavatory was beckoning me. Unfortunately, there did not seem to be anyone about, so I undid my cot and made my way into the hallway. The bathroom was situated at the other end of the flat, and when I got there, I found the passage barred by the living room door which, for some inconsiderate reason, had a door handle well beyond my reach.

I gathered all three books that the family owned, and piling them one on top of the other, I climbed up. Still the problem persisted and, as any toddler would do under those circumstances, I pulled down my pants, deposited my offering at the foot of the offending door, and went back to sleep beside my crime.

In my defence, my calls of 'Mummy, mummy!' had gone unheeded, and I had no notion of what might follow. My mother at last returned, and opening the door from the other side, smelled and then saw what I had done and went ballistic. That last phrase was not in use in those days, but it sums up the situation far better than 'she got angry' which, in her case, would always have been an understatement.

Being the object of her fury didn't bother me as much as the sight of the wide-open French windows overlooking the garden. Apparently, they had not been closed while she was away, and I had been totally alone. The doodlebugs may have terrified me when I was a baby at Wetherall Drive in Stanmore, Middlesex, but this new sense of insecurity was one of the first real worries of my childhood.

I don't recall much after that until my first haircut at the hairdressers. Evidently, I wasn't there to have my hair cut. I was there because the man wanted my ears, my nose, in fact, anything that he could cut off with his scissors. I screamed and screamed at his obvious evil intent.

I had been seated on a short wooden plank placed across the arms of the seat and then enrobed in a huge white cape. It was obvious. I was definitely going to be sacrificed, and to make matters worse, he was going to make me watch it all in the big mirror in front of me. Haircut over and with an embarrassed father, I would call that day an unmitigated success.

A favourite holiday destination for my parents was Walton-on-the-Naze near Clacton. In the late forties and early fifties, it still looked like a bomb site with the remains of wartime defenses still quite evident. Bits of barbed wire were everywhere, as were red 'Danger' notices warning of the debris scattered around the beach.

We had a favourite spot which we visited more than twice, and it was there that I discovered in the sand the ideal seat on which to perch while we had lunch. It was a metal hump standing four or five inches out of the sand, the tail fins only just visible. It was a fairly large bomb which had failed to explode and had not yet been dealt with by the army. But it made a jolly good seat for a small boy, although it did get a little too hot to sit on when the sun was high.

It was there for at least another two years but had been finally removed when I returned some eight or nine years later. A question that has often come to mind is that my father had been in the RAF during the war, so why didn't he recognise a bomb when it was sitting directly in front of him? A normal reaction, one would think, would've been to move away just in case. The other question was, when a beach was so heavily visited by holiday makers each summer, why was such a large hunk of metal not removed earlier?

The Christmas of my fourth year was the best one I can ever remember. I sneaked out of bed quite early on Christmas morning and squeezed each parcel, one by one, in the little pile that was put aside for me.

One package in particular got me excited. Lying in the heap of crumpled wrapping paper was a brown, furry teddy bear. Sitting him on a chair and feeding him Christmas cake from a teaspoon, I pondered what I should call him. A name then came to me in a flash—I would call him Teddy! An hour or so later, my parents found me still sitting in front of him, chirruping away, the two of us covered in cake crumbs.

Miss Hornby's nursery school on Headstone Drive was great. But the most memorable thing at the school was the glorious colour of Ruth's hair. She was four years old, with the most beautiful copper-gold, perfectly straight hair. I don't remember her ever speaking, but she did come to tea, though it was just once.

My mother had cut the edges off the sandwiches, had picked some daisies from the garden, and placed them in the centre of the table in a little pot. And there we were. The joy of being with Ruth far outshone the reality of that sunny day. She will always be a four-year-old girl with beautiful copper-gold hair, forever silent. What was important to me was that my mother had been really kind and taken great care to make this little event into something special.

The nursery was fun. Children could be sick after lunch, and it would just be cleared up as if it was absolutely okay to puke. We could cover ourselves with paint instead of daubing the cartridge paper, and we were just cleaned up. It was terrific. We had our afternoon nap and our play times; nobody ever got cross. Somebody must have done at some time, but I didn't notice it.

It was during that period that I realised I preferred the company of girls more than boys, and I spent more time playing with them. My brother's behaviour towards me probably influenced that preference. Girls were a little more distant; friendship had to be won. They didn't shout and didn't want to fight (most of them, anyway). They would play quietly and non-competitively, smile, and didn't mind me joining in with skipping rope.

Some parents took exception to me, and on one occasion, Susan Willis' father angrily banged on their kitchen window to call her in when she and I were playing with some pebbles in her back garden. He had been watching for a while and obviously could not contain himself any longer. That was the last time I played with her despite her living only three doors away on Albert Road. Once I was over five, the objections became even more stringent.

At Pinner Park Junior School, it was decided, after complaints from certain parents, to divide the playground into two sections, separating the girls from the boys with a picket fence. I noticed that the sun rarely shone on the girls' section, which appeared to be much smaller than the boys' area. After that, skipping was completely off the agenda.

It was a funny thing, but when it came to skipping communally, boys wouldn't do it because none of them wanted to hold the rope. They all wanted to skip and couldn't grasp the concept of taking turns as girls do. You can disagree, if you like, but that's how it seemed to me. How many of you lads ever skipped together in a group with one long rope chanting, 'salt, mustard, vinegar, pepper'? You don't know what you missed!

Anyway, I'm getting ahead of my tale. Stepping back a couple of years to September 1949, it was the end of summer and time for me to go to the big school, Pinner Park Primary School. Despite the pleasant time I had spent at Miss Hornby's nursery, the prospect filled me with dread. My mother tried to assure me that everything would be fine. My brother, who was in his fourth year there, was to take me. She kissed me goodbye and gently pushed me away. The tears began to stream down my cheeks, and I ran back to her.

My fears turned to abject misery when she pushed me away and screamed, 'Get out of my damned sight!' And so I turned away to meet my fate. My brother did take me, or should I say led me, making sure I was always ten paces behind him and behaving as if I was nothing to do with him.

My first few days at infants' school were not happy, but the teacher did her best. Her work was a trial of her patience, always trying to put a bright face on the day despite our grim, miserable little faces and our lack of interest in being appeased. She decided the best therapy was to get us to try and tie our plimsoll laces, which I believe was the turning point.

The school was situated on the edge of the local park, fittingly dubbed by us kids as 'the park', but known to outsiders as Headstone Recreation Ground. I lived on the other side of the park, and so I had to pass through the grounds twice daily. As the seasons changed, I became increasingly fascinated by the park's wildlife.

Dinnertime at Pinner Park School was memorable. It was only by sheer luck that the children who ate there were not wiped out. For those who luxuriate in organic food and healthy eating, spare a thought for those waifs who suffered a post-war diet conjured up by some of the worst cooks ever to have been shown a saucepan.

Every Friday, we had fish, or to be more precise, somebody had fish, and it wasn't us children. We were given fish skins in batter, and no matter how closely we examined the things, there was never the least trace of fish. If somehow one could dispose of the slop, it was a lucky break because the dinner-duty teachers had eyes like hawks and would readily fly into a rage at any child making the attempt. They would stand over the unfortunate little one until every morsel of mushy, batter-fried integument had been devoured.

Another speciality served up was Thursday's heart, complete with ventricles jutting out. It was enough to make us sick just to look at it—pinkish grey with white piping. Gristle stew was Tuesday's delight. No matter how long one chewed, it would never break down. At best, one could swallow it whole if the pieces weren't too big. This delicacy came with mashed swede. The combination was distinctly vomit-inducing, and I've never been able to eat mashed swede since.

I don't remember seeing proper greens, which suggests that they didn't exist on our menu. Those children who had a green card or an orange card meant that they were on special diets—vegetarian, Jewish, or just ill. Oh, how they were envied! Never did so few fare so well.

Though my family were not devoutly religious, I was aware of certain devotional practices. For years, I thought that the word 'amen' at the end of a prayer was another way of saying 'our men', a kind of acknowledgement of those who died in the Second World War. My favourite song was 'All Things Bright and Beautiful'. For me, it was a song full of sunshine, butterflies, and happiness, regardless of the religious element, and I was always pleased to sing it with unbridled gusto in assembly.

Each week, my class would stand in the school hall for a music lesson in front of two teachers— Miss Cheeseman who played the piano and Miss Wetmore to conduct. The hall was situated at the back of the school and overlooked the playing field through long, multi-pained windows. On this particular day, the sun shone brilliantly upon the brightly faced children. What could be a better time to sing 'All Things Bright and Beautiful'?

And so we started, all of us putting our hearts and souls into our cacophonous rendition. Suddenly, it all stopped.

'That boy there! Stop looking out of the window!'

All of us children looked around to see who the culprit was. The voice reiterated the command in an angrier tone, and again, we all looked round.

'Look, he's still doing it!'

The pianist then rose to join her companion, and the two of them screamed into the melée of frightened children. At last, unable to contain their lust for vengeance any longer, they sallied forth into the throng, only to settle their talons on me.

As one shook me like a rag doll, the other slapped my face. I was then dragged out to stand in a corner with my hands on my head. I was so angry, I tried to conjure a spell on them, hoping they would die.

It was a couple of months later, when one of the two became seriously ill and the other had to leave to look after her, that I felt vindicated, and 'All Things Bright' was reinstated to my top ten.

In 1952, Emil Zatopek had won an Olympic Gold Medal for running faster than the speed of light. He was my hero. At eight years of age, being very light with quite long legs, I found that I could run as if gravity didn't apply to me. It was with a spirited endurance that set four of us to run around the largest field in the park, lap after lap, hour upon hour. Other kids, not understanding this extreme obsession, were nonplussed.

How us eight year olds kept going, I don't know. My closest friend, David Addiscott, was still at it after I'd quit for lunch. Years later, I tried the distance around the field walking briskly and found that it took twenty-three minutes to do one circuit.

Running fast became my favourite sport, and Eric Smith, Michael Ashworth, and I were the fastest runners in the school. In the summer, when we were allowed onto the school playing fields, the three of us were always running or racing against each other. It was then that I learned to love the rush of the wind, the sheer dizzying speed, and the dynamic power that this activity generated. Years later, this ability would save my life.

Eric and I were uniquely matched. It was usually impossible to judge who won a race, but Michael, who unfortunately had to win, would never accept the result if it wasn't in his favour. It didn't matter anyway because all we did was run the race again. To give him his due, he did win sometimes, but his disagreeable and aggressive attitude cost him our friendship, for what it was worth.

On the way home after school, Eric and I would walk through the park. One warm, sunny afternoon, we detoured around the edge of the duck pond. It was not really a pond but a moat surrounding an old manor house from which the park gained its name. We stopped at a gap in the bushes that edged the pond. Eric scrambled up an old hawthorn tree whose branches overhung the water by some considerable distance. Having settled on the stoutest and longest branch, he called down to me, 'Come on up here. It's great!'

The words were barely uttered when, in traditional cartoon style, there was a loud crack as the branch gave way, and Eric, in a horizontal position, plunged into the thick, black, slimy water. The ripples ceased, and there was no movement that I could see. He had vanished completely.

I knew that there was nothing that I could do to save him, and as the seconds passed, I pondered what I should do. Suddenly, the slick parted and, as if by some magic that had caused the pond to reject him, he was spewed out, still in a horizontal position, into the light of day. In those minutes, the evil water faeries had transformed him into the creature from the black lagoon, and with amazing speed, he scampered across the top of the water and up the bank to where I was standing.

For me, the moment was one of relief and amusement, but for Eric, after looking down on himself, it was one of anger and horror. He was black from head to foot except for the whites of his eyes. By this time, he was crying, not surprisingly having drunk of the murky pond, but I just couldn't stop laughing. He was the funniest creature I had ever seen. He would only have been funnier had he had grown a tail. It was also the first and last time that I ever saw a human being running on water. Just goes to show that nothing is impossible.

We returned to my flat where he was cleaned up and given a change of clothes before going home. Later that summer, I left Pinner Park School and did not see him again for about twelve years when he visited me in Hastings.

I spent some time in the Cubs while I was at primary school and became interested in knives. It was no wonder since so many of the scouts had either Swiss-army or sheath knives attached to their belts.

It was on the way home with a couple of other Cubs one evening, that we went into an ice-cream parlour in Wealdstone. Behind the tall bar was a young Italian, about eighteen years old, who was carelessly picking at the palm of his left hand with the tip of a double-edged knife, seemingly unaware that his hand was slowly oozing blood. Casually, he asked us if we wanted to buy it from him for five shillings.

Where on earth could I get five shillings?

The blade was six inches long with a broad, double edge tapering to a fine point. The hilt was of the common type made up of rings of compressed leather. I was quite impressed with this beautiful weapon. It was actually the first dagger I had ever seen.

A few months later, as my tenth birthday was approaching, I found a shop in Wealdstone that had a knife of the same type displayed in its window. It was eighteen shillings, and I thought if I got money for my birthday, I might have enough to buy it.

The day came, and I managed to cajole my father into coming with me to the shop, and there I became the proud owner of the beautiful knife.

It was not long before this weapon got me into trouble. I had started to take it into the park with me, stuck down one of my long Cub socks. One particular day, two girls from my class came into the goat field next to the pond and saw me throwing the knife into a tree.

They said nothing to me, and I thought nothing more of it until Monday morning, when I was escorted to the headmaster's office by a teacher, which was rather strange. The headmaster's questioning was calm and nonthreatening.

'Do you possess a dagger?'

'Yes,' I replied.

'Do you take it into the park sometimes?'

'Yes.'

'Do you wear it inside your sock?'

'Yes,'

"Do you chase people with it?'

'NO!'

'Did you chase two girls from your class and threaten to stab them, making them run away crying?'

'No,' I said in astonishment.

'Are you lying?'

'Certainly not!' And thus, the interrogation ended.

The headmaster somehow appeased the girls' parents. The police had been called and were told that everything had been resolved, and that was that. I was dumbfounded. Not a word had passed between the girls and myself, and here I was accused of such a fib, carried forward to the extent that they cried in front of their parents to give some substance to the allegation. How could they do it?

I was very lucky that the headmaster believed me because I think that the odds were well stacked against me. I did, however, promise not to take the knife into the park again, and I swapped it shortly after for an old BSA air rifle...but that's another story.

As I mentioned earlier, I always liked the company of girls, and as I reached the ripe old age of eleven, that inclination became more acute. I now recognise it was a fickle and wayward thing manipulated by mere whims.

And so it was with the beautiful Pat Fuller from North Harrow. She was kind, thoughtful, and considerate. She would write letters to me from Tunbridge Wells during the summer holiday—no one else had ever written to me—and, at the time, she was my one and only friend. She used to help her next-door neighbour with washing the bed linen after one of the children had wet their bed. She had such a generous nature, and I loved being with her.

When her birthday arrived, she invited several of us children from school to her birthday party. Alas, amid the group was a green velvet dress with a broad black satin ribbon around the waist. I could not resist this dress, and the girl inside it immediately became the centre of my attention. Sadly, I neglected the lovely Patricia for the rest of the evening. It was a silly thing to do because my passion for the other girl soon waned once the party was over, but I lost my friendship with Pat.

I met Patricia once more in a pub seven or eight years later. She seemed disillusioned and unhappy as observed through the bottom of a beer glass.

Then there was the lovely Jocelyn Levander. She was in a different class at school, and at the time, I didn't really know her. However, she invited me to her birthday party round about Christmas time after one of the other boys was unable to attend.

What impressed me was how civilised and calm her family seemed, a far cry from my own. It was about five years later that I really came to know her, and she became a close, unambiguous friend. Sadly, we lost contact when I turned twenty.

The boy who had dropped out of the party lost most of his school friends through a boast that fell far short of his expectations. His brother worked at an abattoir, and during half term, he had invited the youngster to visit him at work. As a special treat, the boy was handed a knife, which he plunged into a live pig, and taking such delight in the sensation, he thought that he would share it with us. Everybody in our group was horrified, and it became difficult to have any further contact with him as a result.

During the following year, we all took our eleven plus. I failed, and as nearly everyone in my class had passed, I lost contact with all but a few of the children from Pinner Park Primary School.

3

Seven Albert Road was a garden flat situated about halfway between North Harrow and Wealdstone. It was not really a suitable place in which to bring up a family. There was only one real bedroom, the second being a box room directly underneath the lavatory of the flat upstairs. It had a reasonable lounge, a kitchen, and a bathroom, the latter leading straight off the kitchen. There was also a pleasant, small garden with the advantage of a large black shed.

It would have been ideally suited for a couple but a rather tight fit for four. Although there are people living in far worse situations, I can say from the outset that we should have moved when the opportunity arose. The main problem for me was the rest of the family. They were just all too close.

From about four years of age, my place in the family had started to evolve. My brother had already pushed me, face first, into a bed of stinging nettles. He then resolved that I should undergo neck lengthening. While I was seated on the floor, he placed his hands over my ears, and lifting me to an upright position with my feet dangling, he swung me back and forth. This was a fairly painful process which lasted for as long as his strength could sustain it and despite my shrieks to stop.

On several occasions, he also tried to gas me. Throwing me to the floor, he pinned me down, manoeuvred his backside over my face, and farted. Seeing my disgusted reaction amused him so much, that he repeated this offensive manoeuvre whenever he got the chance. When he ran out of gas, he'd rise and kick me in the ribs just once, just to show me who was the boss.

My brother did not like to share anything with me. The thing which rankled me the most was that after having taken everything he could, he would turn and chant, 'Blue eyes get all the pie, brown eyes get none'. Having been used with such frequency, the phrase eventually became incredibly boring. The best thing about my brother in those early days was his absence, and it didn't really change over the years.

He had forgotten all about 'Jacqueline Stanley' and renamed me 'Belsen Barry' on account of my extreme thinness. The man upstairs always called me 'Biscuit' and would give me sixpence whenever he saw me. It has never been clear in my mind why he called me that. After giving it a great deal of thought, I could only surmise that it was for one of three things: One, I was always eating a biscuit; two, I always asked him for a biscuit, or three, I smelled like a biscuit.

Mrs Booker and her daughter, Pauline, lived two doors up the road from us. They were not very well off but managed to get by. Their dog was well looked after and even had his own sack of dog biscuits. Some were beige, some green, and others were dark brown. There didn't seem to be too many dark brown ones, possibly because I helped him eat them. I felt sure that they were the same as bourbon biscuits, my mother's favourites, but without the filling. I was not a connoisseur of biscuits at six years of age, but they didn't seem too bad, just a little bit dry and hard.

I arrived one morning at Mrs Booker's kitchen door and asked for a biscuit. She looked at me puzzled. I pointed at the sack.

'Can I have a brown one, please?' I asked.

She obviously thought I wanted it for a dog, but when I started to eat it, she cried out, 'What do you think you're doing? That's a dog biscuit. It's bone meal. You can't eat that!' She hurried me out the door and told me to go home.

The dog also had a good thing going with meat. He had his own huge block of green, slightly iridescent, whale meat. It was stained green to stop people from eating it. I thought that was a good idea but wondered why they didn't do the same with his biscuits.

It was around this time that my family went to the circus. It was a Bertram Mills affair, with various whimsical entertainers lining the passage to the big top.

I thought the show was a little boring, particularly the white-faced clown. I think I was a little too young to appreciate the exaggerated slapstick stunts, but when the ringmaster declared that Coco was coming round to all the children during the interval, I perked up. Yes! I was thirsty, nearly parched. A nice cup of cocoa would hit the spot.

What a disappointment. Once again, I felt cheated. I was sure all the other kids got some cocoa, so why didn't I?

'I want some cocoa,' I howled. My parents didn't know what to do. Neither did Coco.

As with the dark ages between the fifth and eighth centuries, so it was with my dark years between ages five to eight. It was a time of my absorption into the scheme of things, when I was shaped from infancy into a self-aware boy. It's when I became conscious of the world around me, developed empathy, and learnt to respond to the suffering of others. It was also a time for learning to handle the challenges life threw at me.

At assembly in our little school, the headmaster warned us of the dangers that lurked in the park. A little girl had been murdered in a park on her way home from her school nearby, and we were advised not to hang around but to go straight home after lessons.

It was mid-winter, dark and scary. What was more frightening to me was not the park but my home. In the hallway was a cupboard under the stairs to the flat above. In that cupboard lurked a monster that ticked, and the stairs would creak for no apparent reason. Never was an explanation proffered for these phenomena at that time, though I later found out that it was the gas meter making the sound. But in my impressionable mind, I believed that the murderer of the little girl and his accomplices were in there, waiting for my return from school.

The backdoor to the flat was always left unlocked so I could get in. With nerves rattling, I entered the kitchen, then into the half-light of the living room, and there they were, ticking and creaking, ready to rush out and grab me.

It was pouring rain and getting darker every minute. I fled from the house and ran to the telephone box in the next road. There was always a light in the box, and I felt comparatively safe there.

Not many people had telephones in those days, so there was a regular stream coming and going. As each person came to use the telephone, I would step outside into the rain and wait for them to finish. It was also a place from which I could observe the main road for my brother's return home on his bike.

By eight o'clock that evening, about twenty people had used the telephone. In the four hours I spent there, I suppose I had stood in the pouring rain for at least an hour, and I was absolutely soaked through. Of the people who came to the box, not one person asked why I was waiting there soaking wet.

At last, some people who lived opposite the telephone box alerted my parents that I had been seen loitering there in the rain. My father eventually came to collect me. To this day, I am still unsure whether or not they had even thought to look for me. The incident was never mentioned.

After that incident, the back door was always firmly locked, and I had to call on a neighbour to let me in with a spare key. The gas meter was explained, and my fear of the cupboard under the stairs dissipated.

But the cupboard remained a place of mysteries. Within it was another little door I could only just crawl through. I found a few of my father's treasures stored there—a violin in its case with a bow and a pair of tennis rackets were the first things that attracted my attention. Inspecting the rackets, I wondered, How could my parents play tennis with these heavy frames on them? I thought they might be some special device to help them win.

Like any small boy finding a musical instrument, I failed to make any sense of it. All I could do was make horrible screeching noises, and after a while, I lost interest.

Unable to find anything worthwhile to do on one school holiday, I decided to re-enact a classic cartoon sketch using the violin. Tucking the chin part of the instrument under my chin, I proceeded to make an altogether different sound. It was like the harsh grating of a saw cutting through taut, thin boards.

After a short while, the violin split into two pieces, and for some reason, I thought that was really hilarious. I presented the shards to my father on his return from work, thinking he would find it as amusing as I had. He wasn't.

'Do you realise what you've done? You've just ruined my dream of becoming a professional violinist!'

It took all of my gumption not to laugh at his ridiculous rant. The fact was that he hadn't played anything on it since the beginning of the Second World War, about fourteen years in all.

There were other interesting items in the cupboard, in particular, my father's bottle of R. White's Lemonade. Because my father was so mean, I thought that this bottle of pop was kept in the cupboard out of sight of my brother and me so that he could keep it all for himself.

My brother was big enough to have taken it at any time from the shelf, and I thought that, because he always had money, he could buy his own. For me, it was different. Money was not a luxury I possessed. So to remain undetected, each day, I would steal one mouthful of this slightly fizzy liquid and top the bottle up with an equal amount of water from the tap, a real study in prepubescent mathematics.

This went on for about a week or two. At last, seeing that I was the only one drinking the stuff, I asked my father, 'Dad, what are you going to do with that lemonade in the cupboard?' hoping that, in a rare fit of generosity, he might let me have it.

'Oh, you mean the battery acid in the old lemonade bottle. I use it to top up the car battery. Best you don't touch it, son. It's got sulphuric acid in it, and it'll probably burn you.'

I didn't dare tell him that I had been drinking it for almost a fortnight. Miraculously, I never had any ill-effects from it.

Among other things in the hidden cupboard was a dog-eared copy of *Winnie the Pooh*—possibly a first edition but missing its covers and boards—that my mother used to read to me when I was little. Later came a Geiger counter in a lead-lined box, but I never found out how to play with it. It all looked rather boring.

Because the bathroom door was directly next to the kitchen sink, going to the loo became a problem when my mother was doing the washing up. She would listen at the door and bang on it if she could hear me having a pee and scream, 'I can hear you! Stop making that noise. If you've got to wee, do it against the side!'

Unfortunately, this behaviour left me with a slight problem aggravated later by a continual retinue of perverts in public bathrooms. I no longer had the courage to visit a public convenience without studying it for several minutes beforehand to make sure nobody was in it, but this safeguard was not always foolproof.

The bedroom that my brother and I shared was about eight feet long and seven feet wide, barely big enough for two boys. Above us was the loo of the upstairs flat, and when Mr Marshall came home drunk, a regular habit, one could hear him cussing and swearing up there while trying to urinate.

I was about eight when a family moved into the adjacent flat. The husband, Dougie Jepp, was a builder who was constructing two houses in Headstone Lane, not far from North Harrow. The plot backed onto some playing fields owned by Harrow School, the front being in a small crescent protected from the road by a cluster of trees.

Dougie had decided he'd keep one house for his own family and sell the other. As he explained, it was not much more costly to build the second house since all the construction equipment was already on the site.

He and his wife had two children and were fully aware of our lack of space, their flat being identical to ours in size. Because they liked my parents, they offered us the chance to buy the second detached bungalow for the grand sum of £1500 with a 90 percent private mortgage and a required deposit of £150.

My father had inherited from his mother £300 worth of government war bonds, which were in his father's possession. My father loved to make lists of things, like expenses, and set about convincing my mother that we could not afford the extra three shillings and nine pence a week that the mortgage repayment would require.

I remember him gloomily saying, 'A mortgage is a weight hanging round your neck. What if we have to put a new roof on it, what then?'

It was quite clear that he had no intention of going ahead with the deal, which was a very generous offer at that time. His father had refused to hand over the war bonds for a deposit anyway.

A year later, the war bonds were willingly relinquished so that my father could buy another old banger for £150, which has always struck me as being a little fishy. By this time, the war bonds had devalued significantly, so my grandfather had to sell a small house in Lavenham for £75 to make up the difference.

The car, a 1947 Vauxhall 12, lasted about six months before it finally gave up the ghost, and my father sold it as scrap for £10. He was happy that he was off the hook with my mother, and so we remained at Albert Road squashed into the tiny flat.

I met Dougie Jepp years later outside a luxurious house between Pinner and Northwood. He invited me in for a cup of coffee and told me that he could never forgive my father for not taking up his offer, a sentiment that I echoed. Maybe a mortgage would've curtailed his obsession for old cars, but evidently, he had his own priorities.

Dad was happy as a sand boy with his new toy despite his now non-existent nest egg and the family getting no benefit from the spare money except the old car. He took the engine out, polished and ground the valves, fiddled with this, fiddled with that, put the engine back under the bonnet, took the engine out again, polished the cylinder head, put new gaskets on things, put the engine back in—the tinkering was obsessive.

We could always tell when he wanted another toy to play with because there were a series of stock phrases that he'd blurt out while driving: 'Can you hear that? There's a knocking!' or 'The big end's going'. I didn't know what a big end was. I thought it might have something to do with a fat person's bottom and that it was rude of him to make such personal comments about people. Eventually, I came to realise that it was something in the engine and that, if it was gone and he couldn't find it, he'd have to throw the car away.

So the Vauxhall, like all the others, went to the car dealer for £10, only to reappear for £50 on the dealer's forecourt a week or so later. I thought, Why did he pay the Americans at Shelton Grange £150 when he could have bought the car for only £50 here?

Sometimes he could be found fast asleep under his latest acquisition, spanner in hand, fag ash on his cheek. To post a letter, he would always go by car despite the post box being less than one hundred yards away. He would then come back the long way round and likely used half a gallon of petrol in the process.

One of the delights at the end of June was to hear the call of the strawberry vendor as he went street by street on his horse and cart calling, 'Strawb'ry, ripe strawb'ry,' and every year, we would buy a couple of punnets from him.

One afternoon, we all sat round the dining table, each with a bowl of luscious, bright red strawberries and some bread and butter. We started to ravenously devour them one by one. Suddenly, my father's voice boomed, 'Stop gobbling them down!' It was directed at me. 'You've got to eat a mouthful of bread and butter between each bite of your strawberries!'

His reasoning didn't interest me one bit, and I carried on just as before. He went raving mad, which was a great surprise since he was normally a placid man. I was eventually made to leave the table. His notion was that by eating the bread and butter, it would make the strawberries in our bowls last longer. But the way I saw it, what difference did it make?

The outcome was that strawberries no longer had their appeal. The vendor came and went and then came no more. There were always blackcurrants to eat and my all-time favourite blackberries, and those were free.

At other times of the year, the strawberry vendor adopted the guise of the rag-and-bone man and that of the scrap-iron man. Same horse, same cart, the only difference being the calls—'strawb'ry, ripe strawb'ry' became 'rag-a-bone, rag-a-bone' or 'owed iyan, owd iyan' (old iron).

Fate played another card from her pack when the old vendor came down Albert Road just when a friend and I were playing outside. His cries of 'rag-a-bone' had a certain intonation which prompted us to join in.

What with the clattering of the horse's weary hooves on the gravel road, the chortling and giggling of my friend and I, and the gruff disapproval of the street vendor. 'Gorn! Clear orf, will ya!' It was a wonder that I actually heard the rapid tapping at the front window of our flat.

Turning around, my eyes met the glaring grimace of my mother, not smiling but grinning with a kind of leering malice. Beckoning me to the kitchen door at the side of the house, I had a strong suspicion that things were not going to be good. Tears sprang from my eyes as I followed her command.

She had been sweeping the floor when she heard our piping melody and had decided to put an end to it. After all, what would the neighbours think, or what would the world think, or what would God think.

As I approached the door, it swung open, and within an instant, I was jerked inside. Before I could react, I had part of the broom head firmly thrust into my mouth. Swinging me round in the same stance, I was propelled backwards through the flat to my bedroom, where I remained for the rest of the day, my mouth full of dirt and my gums quite sore.

All over Britain, rag-and-bone men have been mimicked by children as a sort of national sport, and probably the worst that ever befell those kids was to have a clod or two of horse dung flung in their direction. So I asked myself, *Why me?* and the only answer I could come up with was that my mother was decidedly quite mad.

My father had an unfortunate propensity for being down-right mean. The frown and consternation on his brow were evident whenever I asked for pocket money after observing my brother receive an increase in his allowance. Having re-luctantly agreed, he would then manipulate my spending in a roundabout way by telling me that I would have to save it to buy my mother a Mother's Day present, or a wedding an-niversary present, or a Christmas or Easter or birthday pre-sent. Not surprisingly, this duty, for that is what it became, was never laid on my brother.

During the summer, my father would don his tennis shorts unabashed by his white, hairless, chicken-skin legs. He'd prance around the garden, tennis racket still in its press, waiting for the young girl who lived in the flat up-stairs to join him. I don't remember him ever wanting to play tennis with either my brother or me, while my mother only seemed to worry about Sunday lunch.

It was around this time, when I was about nine or ten years old, that my mother became more irritable and would fly into rages at the least provocation.

The prime time for these angry outbursts was while she did the ironing on Sunday afternoons. The iron would progressively sweep faster and faster, almost as if propelled by her rising rage. Walking would turn into stomping, all culminating in a demand for more of whatever she wanted, be it money, respect, clothes, jewellery—anything.

I soon learned to leave the room, and if my father happened to arrive at that precise moment, it was certain he'd bear the brunt of it. Despite trying to placate her, her sour mood would continue late into the evening.

My brother was never there to witness mother's irrational outbursts, but the cat often did. Feeling a bit peckish, Tibby might venture into the kitchen for food but had to be agile enough to avoid her flying feet. She did get him once with a hefty kick that sent him sprawling across the kitchen floor and crashing into the cupboard on the other side of the room. Self-control was not on her agenda. Tibby eventually suffered kidney failure, which I now attribute to her rough treatment.

One day, a man appeared at the front door saying to my mother that he had found her address affixed to a lamppost in Hong Kong and thought he might look her up. She was sufficiently flattered to invite this stranger in. Thereafter, I knew him as Uncle Saville. He claimed to live in Pinner and that he was a seaman. Though he appeared infrequently, he would always bring an assortment of presents with him for the family.

He seemed to feel entitled to visit us unexpectedly with his kit bag and a small suitcase, staying a few hours until late, and then disappearing once again. My mother loved flattery, and Saville knew that. In the end, my father unceremoniously asked him to leave and never come back.

When my mother's brother, Uncle John, and his wife, Cath, arrived to stay for a few days, the excitement was so great that the kissing and hugging of siblings seemed endless.

My uncle had a broad Essex accent attached to a very loud voice. He was a company sergeant major in the army and as tough as old boots. He and my mother would spend hours laughing and talking and jigging up and down. When his stay ended, my mother's humour would plummet, and we all knew that we were in for another phase of erratic outbursts.

During the early fifties, my mother had a succession of jobs ranging from housework to shop assistant and till girl, eventually settling down for several years at Kodak. This brought in more money, and with my father taking a better-paid job at Walter Kidde, they increased their spending power to no end. Consumerism came to Number Seven, Albert Road, but not contentment.

My brother and I had narrow bunk beds, a wardrobe, and a matching chest of drawers. The door to our room had to be removed because the chest prohibited it from opening. A curtain was put up in its place, and any notion of privacy, peace, and quiet was lost.

The one thing I did get from this new wealth was a bicycle. My brother had a Hobbs racing cycle, which he boasted was handmade, and all of my friends had bikes with drop handlebars and derailleur gears. My bicycle was a Triumph tourer, complete with three gears, straight handlebars, and a carrier on the back for my shopping basket. It weighed about four times more than anybody else's bike. But it was a bike, and after some modifications, it looked a little more acceptable except for the three speed gears, but it served its purpose for a few years.

I shouldn't complain, but it was rather old-fashioned and unexciting. It was the sort of thing my father would buy to keep me in my place and on track for his future plans.

4

Insects started to make an impression on me from a fairly early age, starting with an encounter in our back garden with a wasp wearing an overcoat. The overcoat was actually a jam sandwich with crusts.

As I peeled back the top slice, my attention was briefly distracted and into the sandwich popped the wasp. He did not expect to be bitten, nor had I expected to be stung, so we were both surprised.

Of this event, I can remember little. The pain got the better of me and shut down my brain, and the world stood still. In fact, I don't even remember spitting the insect out. As the years drifted on, I was stung on a regular basis, but despite this, I became a defender of the wasp as being an important player in nature's scheme. It is a kind of pest regulator, environmental cleansing officer and, at times, pollinator. As such, I avoid doing anything to their detriment whenever possible.

Some of the most beautiful creatures are insects. Some have a fragile beauty, others can be dramatic, and then there are those which are majestic. And so it is with an everlasting regret that my first encounter with a member of the last group should have ended in a mini tragedy.

It was an average overcast day at the entrance to our local park, Headstone Recreation Ground. A small brook ran from behind the adjoining houses through a cluster of elm bushes and into a little pool beneath an old hawthorn tree beside the road.

I had borrowed David Addiscott's cowboy pistols and holsters, but being without caps, I busied myself shouting, 'bang, bang' at everything—bushes, trees, water, cigarette ends—when suddenly, out of the bushes, came darting backwards and forwards a magnificent iridescent blue green dragonfly. Shouting 'bang' at it didn't work, so when it disappeared into the thicket, I threw first one, then the other of my pistols into the bushes after it. Nothing appeared, and all was quiet—no hum, no buzz. With trepidation, I crept up to retrieve the toy pistols.

To my amazement and everlasting shame, there was the corpse of the lovely dragonfly, and on top of it, as if somebody had carefully lain them there, were the two pistols with barrels crossed forming an X. This creature was just so incredibly beautiful.

Remorsefully, I carried it home and dipped it in oil, hoping that it might keep its beauty that little bit longer. Unfortunately, after a few days, it became a soggy, greasy, dull mess, and I buried it in the garden.

After that, my attempts to kill flying insects came to an abrupt end. However, this did not stop insects from trying to kill me, or so I thought.

Further into the park, there was a boggy area by the side of another brook in a cutting just below the children's play area. Armed with a twig, I squatted down in my short trousers and probed the mire to discover the devils and mysteries which lived there.

Seeing a water scorpion for the first time was quite a daunting experience. The long tail spike and pincer claws were more menacing than anything I had ever encountered in the natural world. Along with the other creatures which squirmed towards my fingers, its claws were ready to claim anything that might come into its path.

Some few weeks later, while trying to cross the mire by walking along a fallen branch, I lost my balance and sank waste deep into the foul-smelling slick. My mind shot back to the water scorpions, and terrified of being eaten alive, I had what is generally termed 'a little accident'. Fortunately, as I scurried home, the mud concealed my incontinence, and once indoors, I washed myself off and cleaned up my underwear which I put back on, still wet.

I have always been curious about birds. They are, after all, the only warm-blooded creatures, besides bats, which can fly and have such beautiful songs that it is hard to ignore them.

In my first years at junior school, I used to walk part of the way home along the bottom of the ditch in the park, its high sides concealing me as I wandered along. It gave me a strange sense of being part of the wildlife, seeing yet unseen, as I padded over the stones and clay.

It was on such an adventure that I came upon the tiny, freshly dead corpse of a male Great Tit. It was such a find, its vivid colours—yellow, blue, and black—still bright, and I wondered how it came to be lying at the bottom of this gully apparently untouched.

Carefully, I carried it home and decided that it needed to be buried in a little coffin. In the big black shed at the bottom of the garden, amongst all my father's rubbish, I discovered the perfect container, an old tobacco tin. Taking a trowel, I interred this gem of nature's perfection in a small hole and scattered some daisies over it before covering it over with soil.

About three weeks later, my curiosity became too great to cast off, and I disinterred the little creature. To my horror, the stench that reached my nose was diabolical, and when I saw the hundreds of maggots swimming in fluid amongst the matted feathers in a manic agitation, I was completely repulsed. I quickly replaced the lid and promptly reburied the poor thing.

I suppose this was my first realisation of the nature of things and that, in the end, those of us who choose burial will meet no better fate. 'Ashes to ashes. Dust to dust. If the fire don't get us, the maggots must.'. But that is the way of things, and the world will carry on without us...we hope.

I spent weeks after that seeking out rare species of birds and insects but rarely saw anything. However, one day a year or so on, David Addiscott, his younger brother, Will, and I discovered in the allotments next to the goat field, a veritable monster caterpillar climbing the tall weeds. It had large eye markings about four inches long, was as fat as a farmer's finger, and waved its front end around in a most disagreeable manner.

Full of bright ideas, I recalled my father's Box Brownie camera and declared that such an animal needed to be photographed. David and I raced off to get the camera, which probably had no film in it anyway, leaving Will to keep an eye on the thing until we returned.

We were back within a few minutes, only to meet Will running as if the gates of hell had opened in front of him. White with terror, he shot past us and shouted, 'It moved!' David and I searched for about half an hour, but the monster had gone. It was an elephant hawk caterpillar and was obviously camera shy.

One of my greatest achievements as a small boy was to fill a pillowcase with feathers. I am dead serious here. I gathered feathers wherever I went and spent hours trying to identify which type of bird had lost a particular feather. Some might say that this was a good, mind expanding exercise; others might claim, 'That kid is stark-raving mad!' But most people just looked at me with a kind of withering sympathy, as if to say, 'Oh, he can't help it. He's just too thin.'

My favourite feather of all time was the little curly one which could be seen on the rump of a drake mallard, and believe me, it is quite a hard one to come by.

Odd behaviour in the family was not my prerogative either. Our cat Tibby was quite a gentle soul but found it necessary to prove to me that he was interested in birds too. One morning, he trotted down the garden path and proudly presented me with the desiccated body of a green finch, as if offering a contribution to my feather collection. I thanked him profusely and waited for him to go to sleep before depositing it in the dustbin.

On another occasion, he came galloping in through the kitchen door with a live sparrow, which he immediately tried to push through the bars of our budgerigar's cage. I think it was meant as a companion gift to Tweety Pie. After all, the budgie did sit on his head every evening while he watched the television. As for the sparrow, it survived the ordeal and flew away, apparently unscathed.

5

My family used to visit my paternal grandparents occasionally at their house in Lavenham during my childhood, and what struck me quite early on about the village was, *What a strange place*. It was not so much the sight of a village in a state of decay as it was the rank odour in the air. It was like opening an ancient coffin and inhaling deeply the last exhaled breath of the dead.

On the sunny summer days that we visited, I used to feel so tired that I would wander down to the cemetery and doze off amid the stones for an hour or two.

Lavenham is no longer what it was in the early fifties. Gone are the tumble-down wrecks of medieval houses with broken roofs and rotting timbers. Gone are the little shops selling vegetables and baskets. Gone is the milk lady with her horse drawn chariot, carting churns of milk and drawing jugs full as she called door to door around the village. Gone is the railway station and the signal box in which my grandfather worked. It is all traffic and tourism now. All the ancient houses have been restored or rebuilt with little sign of the poverty that once festered in so many of the small Suffolk towns at that time.

During the first decade of the twentieth century, my grandmother was a Lavenham girl with dark eyes and long black hair. It was a far cry from the wraith-like figure that had crept across the front room and climbed reluctantly into a truckle bed set in an alcove in the wall, the only time that I can remember seeing her. She was slowly dying from leukaemia, and though still only in her fifties, she had lost every sign of her youth. She was clad in a long white shift, her white hair hanging lifeless and unkempt below her shoulders and her skin already dead white and bloodless.

I saw the same figure again at a slightly later date, following the same route but stopping for a few seconds alongside my grandfather in the middle of the room.

Decades later, I learnt from my mother that the figure I saw did not have the physical attributes of my grandmother and there was no truckle bed in the wall, only a shallow cupboard. I conjectured that the figure was possibly a spirit from an earlier time, likely an inhabitant from the house that existed before my grandparents' home was built.

My grandmother had over-nurtured my father to the point that he would run back from the schoolhouse at the age of seven for 'titty bar'. I sometimes wondered if other lads were doing the same thing after school. One could imagine that, instead of the cries of kids playing in the street, all one would hear every afternoon at three forty-five would be the contented sucking noises of large infants attached to their mothers' breasts.

My grandfather had no liking for me, and I would fairly describe him as a miserable old sod. To prove my point, one Sunday morning after an overnight stay, I greeted him cheerily with, 'Good morning, Granddad!'

His instant response was to take off his Sam Brown belt and threaten me with it. 'Don't you talk to me!' he growled, and off I ran down to the cemetery.

My father's half-brother, Stanley, having been disposed of at such an early age, became known in my family as 'the bastard', a title which he held until his death. Stan and his wife, Marjorie, were really nice people, kind, well-meaning and generous. They lived next door to my grandparents in a small house left to Stan by his uncle on my grandmother's side, much to the aggravation of my grandfather, who never spoke to them for over forty years.

They had a son a couple of years younger than me, and over-compensating for Stan's early loss of a mother and family home, they tended to spoil him, not that it took any toll on the boy's future prosperity.

I can recall, with a curious revulsion, the sight of him sitting on his mother's lap in their car, sucking a woollen doll's arm as we drove along. He was at least twelve years old. Unfortunately, this heavily coloured my attitude towards him, especially when my father sneered at me with quips like, 'Look what a failure you are. Look at how clever your cousin is.' My dislike of the little lad became more entrenched as time went on and is still with me to this day.

When my grandmother died, an event that my parents never shared with me, she had left Stan and Marjorie a small plot of land across the road in Lavenham High Street, which my father forever viewed with jealousy.

'That should have been my parking plot, not that little bastard's. He parks his car on it, and it should have been mine. I have to park out in the street while the bastard has got that.' This was a continual complaint and was echoed time after time when we visited Lavenham.

But, of course, this was just between us. To Stan's and Marjorie's faces, my parents were as sweet as could be, even inviting them to stay at our flat in North Harrow, which they did with their son on a couple of occasions despite the cramped accommodations.

After my grandmother died, Stan and Marjorie went out of their way to be generous to my grandfather. Every day, they took round to him a midday meal and made sure that he lacked nothing. Their kindness knew no bounds, and to all intents, it appeared that the ancient rift had at last been repaired. But when Hetty, an old flame from before the First World War came back into my grandfather's life, without any sign of gratitude, the old swine re-instated his animosity towards them.

Both Stan and Marjorie were heavy smokers, the fag ash perpetually falling down their fronts. They were never seen without a cigarette dangling from their mouths, even while in the kitchen, and in time, Marjorie developed cancer and died. It was a terribly sad day.

My grandfather finally went off to meet his maker, someone with horns, I should think. He was followed by his then wife, Hetty, within a few days. My parents had somehow coerced Hetty on her deathbed to change their joint will.

Originally, my brother and I were to be the main beneficiaries, provided Hetty died within a week of my grandfather's death, which I believe she did. We would have inherited the house in Lavenham, but my mother declared, 'We aren't going to miss out this time!' and they duly received, more or less, everything that the old couple had possessed.

When they moved into their newly acquired residence, Stan went to welcome them, but standing on the doorstep, my mother proudly declared, 'I'm a woman of property now. Go away!' and shut the door in Uncle Stan's face. My mother was pleased to recount this incident as if it was the righteous thing to do.

Rifling through the house contents, they discovered that a certain wardrobe was locked, and breaking it open, they found handbags full of five-pound notes. As my mother threw the money into the air in celebration, my father lost his composure, punched her on her arm, and shouted, 'It's all mine!'

It was more than probable that the money wasn't rightly theirs. Apparently, Hetty had insisted before she died that the wardrobe was to be given to one of her relatives.

My brother and I did inherit from the estate. We both received a cheque for £347 each. The problem with that was that the solicitor sent mine to my brother and his to me. I telephoned my father to ask the solicitor to correct the error, a simple task, but was met with an angry tirade: 'All this is costing me money!'

My grandfather had accumulated a vast quantity of odd bits and pieces during his life, mainly derived from the lost property office at Lavenham station. In a pretence of generosity, my father handed to me from this hoard three broken silver pocket watches for me to play with because, as he said, 'They aren't worth anything'. One was quite ordinary with a simple movement and a broken hair spring, but the other two had chain-driven fusee movements, and with a little lubrication, they both came back to life.

Being in the antiques trade by this time, I sold them as a lot to a watch dealer, and thinking that my father might have been pleased that I had made some use of them, I thanked him. He nearly cried and would have torn out all his remaining hair, but he just managed to hold himself together, even though his face spoke volumes. His ill-concealed anger clouded the day for several hours. Everything else, including some things that I thought should have been shared out, he knocked out to a dealer for pennies rather than let the family have them.

It was sometime later, overwhelmed by his own generosity, that he telephoned us declaring, 'How would you like a thousand pounds?' The catch was that he was offering to loan us the money at ten per cent per annum, which at a higher rate than the current Barclay loan interest. His beneficence was so astounding that we declined the proposal while at the same time trying to refrain from choking.

There is a great deal more about my parents' time in Lavenham over the next few years of their lives, but it is outside the focus of my history and more to do with theirs. It is unlikely that anyone will ever write it down, and so it will pass away like so many other untold tales, good and bad.

6

Most parks have a children's playground, and Headstone Recreation Ground was no exception. In the 1950s, there were no fences or gates around the play area, just a hedge through which all the kids used to run. Besides having a notice saying that big kids weren't allowed on the swings, there was a high slide, a monkey climb, a bell-shaped roundabout, a seesaw, swings, and a drinking fountain overlooking the boggy place where I had my 'little accident.' There was also a devilish contraption, much like a battering ram, seating about ten, which hurtled backwards and forwards and which took the life of a young girl and was promptly dismantled.

Very nearly all the children that I knew had, at some time, taken a whack on the head from a swing or fallen off a swing, and I certainly was not to be left out. One of the great tricks of the day was to get the swing to fly as high as it could go, then jump off at the ultimate height. It was a strangely scary and often dangerous feat which lasted for a short period, with most of the enthusiasts finding the landing not as interesting as the flying.

In those early days, it was the rubber padding under the equipment that helped me survive moderately unscathed. I think the swings got me about three times, but a more memorable occurrence took place on the roundabout. This was an octagonal, bell-shaped construction suspended on a large central column standing altogether about eight or nine feet high and lined with eight ash benches. Depending on how it was being propelled, it could revolve in an orderly fashion or violently crash from side to side so that the girders that held the benches would scrape around the tarmac. A child could either sit or stand on the seats, but it was necessary in all cases to hang on tight.

So it came to pass that somehow I managed to slip upside down under one of the seats, and as the thing charged round and round and up and down, I had the distinct misfortune of being knocked almost senseless. Not satisfied with doing this once, I performed this amazing trick several times, and it was only after somebody broke a leg underneath the roundabout that my pastime was finally brought to an end. The roundabout was also decommissioned.

To make up for the gradual decline of amusement, the Corporation Parks and Gardens Department had installed a fine new seesaw. It was state of the art and had an amazing pneumatic bump so that, as one end reached the ground, it would instantly jolt itself up again.

It was quite large, with the supports made from heavy steel girders. Not having definitively learned my lesson with the roundabout stunt, I replicated my moronic manoeuvre and clung onto the seat with my legs as I hung upside down from beneath. Down it came with my head as the initial recipient of the tarmac's harsh reception. It was like being pile-driven into the ground, and for good measure, the see-saw delivered that extra thrust to push itself up again. Surprisingly, this episode didn't hurt too much because the tarmac was still soft from the installation and made a splendid impression of my head.

The last head banging took place about a hundred yards from the playground in a field behind the manor house during a cinder-track cycle race. It was a community affair, quite amateurish in its presentation by modern standards, but a really good family day out... for some. The track was set out in a circle and marked off with metal posts linked together with rope.

My brother and I lay on the grass and watched the swirling mass of legs, wheels, and pedals whorl past, throwing up dust and grit into our faces. Was this really a race or was it just big people not finding anything better to do? It really didn't matter as it was just so exciting.

When one of the front runners skidded on the track and fell off his bike, the others, being unable to stop on the cinders, all crashed helplessly into him. Suddenly, as the numbers increased, they were transformed into one huge writhing mass. Then, for some reason, this animated clump of riders and bikes changed direction, and coming back swirling, groaning and lurching, decided to fall on my head.

It all happened so fast that neither my brother nor I had the chance to get up and out of the way. My brother claimed that he got the worst of it because he got a pedal in his ear. That was probably God punishing him.

My injuries were mostly caused by people standing on my face while they tried to extricate themselves from the mess. Later, as my mother led me away, I chanced to look at my reflection in a window and, horrified, saw my face veiled by a curtain of blood. I howled. My mother screamed at me not to make a spectacle of myself and reiterated her usual 'you're showing me up' chestnut.

None of my injuries were serious, just a myriad of minor nicks and some bruising, but it did leave me with a couple of horizontal scars on my cheek which lasted for years. I always thought they gave me a tough persona, until I admitted that they weren't from fighting, but with age came wrinkles, and after a while, the scars disappeared.

Apart from walking into a lamppost or falling off my bike, my head remained relatively intact thereafter as I passed unnoticed from childhood into adolescence.

7

I am a great believer in anything that brings youngsters together in order to learn more about nature and how to behave within the community. After all, it can be great fun... for some.

I joined the Cubs sometime during my ninth year and stayed in the 19th Harrow group until I was about ten and a half. I started at the back of a line of six kids and left just as I was about to stand at the front and become known as a 'sixer'. The whole concept of being in charge of anything or anybody was appalling to me, and along with other considerations, my departure from the pack was made that bit easier.

One of the things which I hated was 'bob a job' week. Some kids would come in with thirty-five shillings, their little cards ticked by all their family members, whereas others might return with twelve shillings and sixpence, their cards ticked by their families and dog.

Entries on these cards would typically read: 'Washed windows—two shillings and sixpence; mowed lawn—five shillings.'

My card would read: 'Removed stones from garden—sixpence', and that would be the only entry because nobody would employ me. One could hear the whispers: 'He's so thin. What if he collapses in the house? It would be our responsibility!' Or was it that they just didn't like the look of me?

The stone removal episode took about seven hours on my hands and knees in the front garden of a house on my street. I had started at about ten in the morning, and around three o'clock that afternoon, a group of kids came by and asked me what I was doing. I told them. Having a spirited communal sense of humour, they scurried around in the road gathering as much gravel as they could to shower me and the half-cleared garden. When the owner of the house returned, she studied the garden for a few moments and declared that it looked much the same as it did before. She handed me sixpence, concluding that I had not done the job properly.

'Look, there's one there, and over there. Can't you see it? There's another one. If you want to get on in the world, my lad, you'll have to do a lot better than this,' she said. It was round about this time that I began to get interested in slavery and felt that maybe I had already found my niche in the world.

The following year, I did slightly better when an old lady in Pinner View, North Harrow, invited me into her house to sort out a biscuit-tin full of playing cards. A few things bothered me, and it took a while for me to accept that I wasn't going to be put in a cage, fattened up, and eaten. She seemed so happy that I had called. It didn't seem natural.

A few questions played around in my head: Firstly, was this really on old lady and not a witch? Secondly, why had she put all these playing cards, mixed up as they were, in a biscuit tin? Is it to hypnotise me? And thirdly, was that cup of tea drugged?'

After half an hour, I had sorted through about half of them while seated at a little baize-topped folding card table in a room which was small and Victorian in decor, with heavy velvet curtains and old ebonised furniture. She opened the door and showed such a charming delight as she brought me some tea and biscuits.

'The packs may not be complete,' she said, which made me think, *What am I doing this for, then?* But I continued, drank the tea, ate the biscuits, brushed the crumbs off the table onto the floor, and within the hour, I had finished.

I had sorted between five and seven packs, each pack sorted into different suits. There wasn't a single complete pack amongst them. I called her to say that I had finished, and she seemed so pleased that she gave me two shillings and said, 'Come back tomorrow because I'm sure that I have other things for you to do.'

I went back the following day, but there was no answer at the door, and then Friday came, and 'bob a job' week was over.

Another episode involved an old scoutmaster who, for some reason, had been given the moniker of 'Monty'. He was from another planet where all these Monties were actually cloned and sent down to earth to lurk around scout huts all around the world. He was dressed in a 1930s scout costume: long baggy shorts below the knee, sagging beige gaberdine belted raincoat, pointed scout hat, woggle, garters around his socks, a few faded badges, and a long walking stick. He was about seventy and was markedly stooped, probably from doing things to little boys that he shouldn't. He looked too much like a bad fairy or an animated Thermagen*.

He had chosen me for 'nurturing', and wanted me to go to Ruislip Woods for a 'ramble' (I think he meant rumble or fumble). It was arranged for a Saturday, and as the days ticked by, I started to have misgivings about this old person. I told my parents that I didn't want to go.

Teeny the troupe leader assured my parents that Monty was all right, and there was nothing for me to worry about. So the day came, and I decided not to go to this rendezvous.

The following week, as I was leaving the scout hut, there was Monty. His hand shot out like lightning and gripped my arm with his horrible horny claws. He led me through Wealdstone High Street, down a side road and into an alley which ran behind the shops.

'Take off your shoes and socks,' he said sharply.

---

*Thermagen. (coll. Fermygim) A species of humanoid creatures, often seen at edges of woodlands on the outskirts of villages and small towns, usually partially hidden by trees. Typically lone, can stand for several hours, often mistaken for a blind person. Not known to vocalise.

'Why?'

'Because it's good for you to walk barefoot.'

'But there's broken glass down here.'

'No, there isn't! Now take your shoes and socks off!' I bent forward as if to do as I was told, but having the legs of a rabbit, I was off like a shot down the alley and back onto the high street.

The following Friday, he was there again. This time, I wedged myself between two other kids, and as he tried to grab me, off I ran. That was the last time I went to the Cubs.

I saw Monty some years later, dressed in the same costume, at the edge of the spinney in the park with a group of youngsters around him. He was showing them his collection of pornographic postcards, and I heard someone remark, 'Eww! He's got his willy hanging out!'

During this time, there was a world-wide jamboree held at Harrow around 1953–54. It was decided by our troupe leaders that I was going to run, and it was important that I did well. I was not happy despite Roy Rogers, his lasso, and Trigger being there.

The day was saved for me by a large and ominous black cloud. There were Cubs and Scouts from every part of the world, all expecting to do their best except for one, who was praying that the sky would open to snatch him up or empty its contents on the festival. It did the latter.

As I stood there soaked through, I heard somebody say, 'It's cancelled.' This should have been excellent news for me, but I often confused cancelled and postponed, and though my immediate terror was averted, I actually thought that I was going to relive it all over again at a later date. Ironically, I asked some grown-ups what cancelled meant but was met with blank expressions. I thought they must have been Germans.

I went on a couple of weekend camps at Sarrat in Buckinghamshire. It was great! At night, we all spread our ground sheets, side by side, under the big central tent. I found a cosy little patch about four inches lower than the surrounding ground to place mine.

As night came, we all slipped into our sleeping bags and went to sleep. Towards midnight, Teeny, Ahkalah, and the rest of the group leaders returned from the local public house in the pouring rain. Being a little less than quiet on their arrival, I awoke to find that my little dip in the ground had become more of a drainage ditch for the rest of the tents and had filled to the brim, with me still asleep in it. Somebody gave me another set of pyjamas, and I spent the rest of the night in with Teeny. I'm just glad that it wasn't with Monty.

The Christmas show was yet another traumatising crucible, what with Scouts dressed up as women, wearing make-up and singing songs like 'Sailing Along on the Crest of a Wave'. It was almost as scary as going to church to sing Christmas carols. I hated it, particularly the exhibitions to show how clever us little nippers were.

Once again, I was faced with another challenge. 'You have to make something original to display in the show.' What could I possibly do? For days I worried about it but no ideas came. In desperation, I tried to draw a kestrel swooping with its wings outstretched, about to catch something. I made three or four attempts, but they all looked just too much like rubbish.

So, the evening before I was to hand in my work. I cheated. I took some grease-proof paper from the kitchen and traced the picture that I had used as my inspiration from a book, coloured it in and, shockingly, won a prize!

'Did you do this yourself?' the judges inquired.

I nodded. I had not only cheated, but now, I had also lied. Why did they have to choose my picture? I didn't ask them to choose it. In fact, I would have rather put nothing into the show, but then I would have been the only one who didn't.

The following year, the same show, same songs, same make-up, the same exhibition and, needless to say, the same dilemma arose. At the last moment, I found a lump of balsa wood, quickly whittled it into a boat shape, daubed blue and red enamel paint over it, and won another prize. The judges must have been mad—the paint was still wet!

The scout hut was about a mile and three quarters from home, and I use to do the last mile by bus. Eventually, I thought it was safer to walk the whole route rather than stay in Wealdstone for any longer than necessary The bus stop was opposite one pub and to the side of another. The one across the main road often had to board up the windows after the Friday and Saturday night brawls. When trouble started earlier than usual, one could hear glass breaking and see bits of furniture flying out of the windows. I decided then that Wealdstone was only safe to visit during the day.

8

My first trip to the dentist at age five was a family affair, with my father as chaperone and my older brother for comic relief, at my expense. The waiting room exuded old-fashioned elegance with oak panelling and leather-seated chairs but oddly featured a stand holding half a dozen billiard cues.

The billiard cues, my brother explained, were for digging out teeth after being fitted with sharp steel gouges on the ends. Alternatively, they could be used for injecting cocaine into a patient's gums. They were, he added, very useful implements that the dentist used on a regular basis. I believed him and could hardly sustain my terror.

A few weeks later, I returned with my father to have six of my milk teeth dug out with billiard cues after being anaesthetised with gas. I knew all about gas. People died from it in the trenches, in their kitchens, and even in their baths. I started to scream as soon as the dentist approached me.

'I don't want cocaine gas. I don' t, don't!' I distinctly remember the dentist struggling to hold the mask over my face while I clawed at his. He resorted to placing his knee on my chest to keep me in the chair until I finally succumbed. I didn't dream of Mickey Mouse as the dentist had promised.

The dentist's parting shot to my father was, 'Don't ever bring that brat here again!' and as we walked to my father's car with my gums feeling like jelly and my mouth full of blood, I thought, Well, that's something achieved. I won't be going there again.

A few years later, the school dentist at primary school declared that I needed thirty-one fillings. Fortunately, my parents had found a new dentist in North Harrow, who checked my teeth over and wrote to the school dentist disputing his assessment. He suggested to us that the man was mad. I ended up with three fillings, too many as far as I was concerned, but a lot better than thirty-one.

I was thirteen when my mother became increasingly convinced that I was growing fangs next to my eye teeth and determined that something had to be done. After all, how could she be seen out with a boy who had grown fangs?

Of course, there could have been a rational thought behind it. She may have actually thought that it might be better for me later in life if my teeth were a little more even. One can only conjecture, but in past records, the jury on that score might have been out for months.

Needless to say, the dentist agreed, and the choice of wearing a brace or going for a specialist consultation at a hospital were the two options offered to me. I had never seen a boy with a brace smoking, so that was definitely out. Therefore, I agreed to see a specialist. The third choice, which was to just forget it, was missing from the menu entirely.

The specialist thought that it was necessary to remove four back teeth, perfectly whole unfilled teeth, in the vain hope that all of my other teeth would move round, giving my fangs a chance to get back in line. I should have opted for the brace because all that happened after four days in hospital was that the teeth next to the new gaps fell over sideways, so that I had little curled splinters of bone surfacing out of my gums for over a year.

The general intrusions to my mouth resulted in my having only two and a half back teeth left. It now seems to me that this was all part of a dental conspiracy to keep dentists working and to prolong their incomes well into their dotage. Imagine a thousand boys all needing dental treatment caused initially by faulty or unnecessary treatment. For the purveyors of such inflictions, it would be a bit like winning the lottery.

There is one thing I will say, however, in their defence. It has come to my attention that many dentists die from cancer. I have a notion that it could be caused by either or both of two things: the drilling into the tooth and imbibing the gas produced by the heat of the drill or the breathing in the fumes of old amalgam used for fillings when they are replaced. But I could well be wrong.

9

The first time I met my maternal grandfather, he was standing behind the bar he managed at the Crown Inn at Lower Dean, about a mile or so from Shelton Grange. He and his second wife lived above the pub. A Raggedy-Ann-like character, he had thinning, long grey hair that was swept back from his brow. His thick, cotton, striped shirt lacked its collar but still sported the studs. His old grey flannel trousers, unbuttoned at the top of the fly, were suspended by a pair of equally ancient leather and elastic braces.

He was quite stooped, and his knuckles displayed considerable arthritic deformities as he clutched his well-used walking stick. It was rumoured that he had been shot during the First World War, but he was more likely to have been suffering from chronic arthritis.

It was around 1950, and the villages in that area still maintained an authentic bucolic feeling. Even the village pump was still in use.

Looking back, the pub had probably not changed for over a hundred years. It was an overall brown colour throughout. The panelled wood counter was about level with my nose, and the customers' loo was on raised ground outside the pub. That was the most modern thing in the whole place. It was a corrugated tin hut about the size of an old telephone box, with just a hole in the ground for its visitors.

I was five years old, too young to understand the trauma of the visit, but I remember my parents' grey faces as they peered at my grandparents' youngest child, Nicholas, who, I later understood, had Down's syndrome.

After the bar had closed at lunchtime, I found my grandfather seated over an old iron cutter in an open barn next to the pub cutting thick rubber and leather soles and heels, piece work for a Nottingham shoe manufacturer. It was a pleasant day—the sun was shining, the swallows flitting in and out above my grandfather's grey head. But for my mother, it was a day of gloom, as if the end of the world had come. It soon passed when she found something else to dissatisfy her.

Five years later, my grandfather and his wife moved into a large, red brick Victorian mansion situated in the middle of the countryside near the Bedfordshire–Northamptonshire border. It was known as Shelton Grange and was located just outside the village of Shelton, not far from the Cat and Custard Public House.

My grandfather, Stanley William Hazelton, had rented the house from a local farmer for a pittance and had promptly sublet part of it to an American family from the USAF base close by. By doing this, he not only covered his own rent but also made a small income from it.

The house was exciting. The massive cellar underneath was clad in marble. There was a dark, narrow stairway leading to the rooms upstairs from the huge kitchen hidden behind what looked like an ordinary cupboard door. A massive billiard room was attached to the side of the house.

Beyond that were more outbuildings where my grandfather kept golden pheasants and a 1930s open-top tourer with a long bonnet, running boards and leather upholstery. There was also an orchard and, at the back of the house, a wall-enclosed farmyard with sties and barns owned and used by the landlord.

After lunch, having done the washing up, my grandfather soaked his thin greyish-white hair in the murky dish water which, I should imagine, would have kept his scalp pretty well greased.

My step-grandmother was an abrupt and seemingly irritable woman, but who could blame her after having had eight children, three of whom were still living at home. So, what with the flies from the adjoining pigsties and the wasps and all the relatives coming and going, it all seemed much like the hub of the universe.

It was my ill fortune to have been sent there each summer holiday for three years running, from the ages of ten to twelve. My brother was at scout camp while my parents did something else. Whatever that was, I never found out. It was obviously an arrangement to get me out of the way.

I was alone most of that time, but it brought me much closer to the world of nature and made me realise that everything in that world needed to be respected.

The first time I was left at the Grange was not too bad once I got over the initial shock of finding that my parents had vanished overnight without any warning. Robbie and Ivan, who were only a few years older than me, were my half-uncles, and their presence and the warm sunny August days made it all the more bearable. The harvest was taken in; the fox sometimes managed to take a chicken; the dog, Chips, sometimes caught a rat, and life continued—for some, that is.

One day, Robbie and Ivan suggested that we should watch out for rabbits in the field next to the orchard while the wheat or barley was being taken in. It seemed to be a good idea at the time.

After about half an hour in the field, a young rabbit broke cover, and we took up the chase. I thought that if I could catch it, I could possibly make it my pet. Running as fast as I could, I drew level with it, and as I reached out to grab it, Ivan's stick thumped into its hind leg, and the poor creature lay there squealing. Its leg was broken. Ivan dispatched it, and crying, I returned with them to the house.

The animal was served up for dinner that evening, and my grandfather told me that, as a special treat, he had put some raisins on my plate. Sure enough, there was a handful of small round objects mixed up among the rabbit, the cabbage, and the potatoes.

I glanced at everyone else's plates as they all sat there grinning at me, and I saw that they had none on theirs. It was then that I realised that my grandfather had laced my food with the droppings taken from the rabbit's intestines. I ate the dinner but left the droppings on the side of my dish.

My grandfather liked playing cards, mainly for money, and I soon learned that I had to keep one eye on the cards and the other on my little pile of half-pennies because every now and then, he would try to distract me with, 'Look at that spider over there!' or some such rubbish and steal a coin or two from my fast-dwindling stack.

When I told my mother about these things, her response was that he always liked to play practical jokes on people because 'he's such a lovable old man and has such a wonderful sense of humour'. Like everything else she told me, I believed her.

As an adult, I have come to understand that laughing at a child's expense isn't humour; it's the cowardly choice of using someone vulnerable to prop up your own fragile sense of worth. It's especially damaging when it comes from someone who's supposed to be a protector.

Robbie and Ivan decided that I was an easy target to terrorise, being younger than they were. In a field next to the house, the farmer kept a pair of placid horses who spent their days munching grass and standing about dreaming, much like any other horse. However, the brothers planted the idea into my impressionable mind that the animals had a predilection for the flesh of small boys. I had already had a brush with a New Forest pony, which seemingly wanted a portion of my face to chew, so I found their words quite believable.

One night whilst returning from Lower Dean in the pitch darkness, the road being illuminated only by the light of their torches, the demonic duo suddenly and silently disappeared into the blackness, leaving me standing on my own in the road. They then started to call out, 'Ain't you frit? Ain't you frit? Ole fox'll getchyer. Look! There's a rat behind yer!' 'Frit' I wasn't, but I was seriously pissed off with the word frit and their stupid bumpkin behaviour.

At bedtime, I was told that I had to sleep with my head under the bedclothes, otherwise the rats which ran about in the bedroom during the night would get onto the bed and gnaw my nose and ears off. And so, with the breaking of each new day, I was relieved to find that I was still intact, same fingers, ears, nose, and toes.

The benefits eventually outweighed the detriments. During the day, I could watch a group of green woodpeckers drumming on a dead tree or beautiful feather-winged moths dancing over the roadside verge. I found mushrooms, long-tail feathers from pheasants, and deserted chicken nests with eggs gone bad. It was all worth the price, or so it seemed that year.

One evening, on the way back to the Grange, we three turned into the driveway of the house. As we approached the rear courtyard, there was a horrific scream, and in the half light, we could just make out the shape of the farm cat running at top speed, hotly pursued by a huge rat which seemed, at that moment, to be gaining on it. Suddenly, there was another horrible scream, and then silence.

Too frightened to investigate the fate of the cat in case the monster rat was still there, we quickly passed into the safety of the kitchen. All that night, I worried about the cat, and in the morning, I hurried out and up the lane to inspect the corpse. But there, to my great relief, was the body of the rat, cleanly killed by a single bite to the back of the neck. There was no sign of the cat, and my relief was not complete until that afternoon when he came wandering past me as if nothing had happened.

It was an interesting couple of weeks, one way or another. I had become more immersed in the natural world and had forgotten that my parents had dumped me there without so much as a goodbye. But not so the following year.

Again, I was left there despite assurances from my parents. As usual, us lads went off to bed, three single beds in a row, but in the morning, I awoke to find the other two beds empty and no sign of my parents either. Downstairs at breakfast, I asked where Robbie and Ivan were and was told that they had gone to pick potatoes. 'When will they be back?' I asked several times, but there was no reply.

Fifty years later, I found out that they had gotten up very early and were sent away to their sisters' homes for the time that I was to be there. Obviously, this was done so that I would not contaminate them with my town ways. However, I was expected to keep Nicky, my half-uncle with Down's syndrome, occupied, which, for a ten-year-old, was neither fair nor easy.

Nicky was a country boy and prone to wander. He was quite at home among the cattle and would regularly disappear into the surrounding fields where he was as happy as the days were long. Physically, he was very strong and mentally, full of guile.

On one occasion, he had gone up to the top of the hundred-acre field amid a herd of bullocks. My grandfather called me to bring him back, a situation which made me feel quite nervous, the bullocks being quite large and I quite small.

I could see Nicky among the cattle about a hundred yards away, waving a long stick around his head. To my right was a narrow coppice separated from the field by a barbed wire fence. The top end of the woodland was not fenced off, and the cattle would often browse in the hedges and trees.

The other side of the coppice was a field about eighty yards wide, which contained the two child-eating horses. After that, there was a low hedge, a ditch, and a wide bed of nettles, altogether taking up another three or four yards and leading to the edge of the road.

As I ran up the field towards Nicky and his companions, I kept all the exit options in my head. Granted the two horses did complicate the issue if things were to go wrong, and, needless to say, they did.

Dear little Nicky, who was about three years younger than I, had managed to martial the bullocks into a line at the top of the rise, and with a vigorous, 'Hoy!' and a swift stroke with his stick on the back of one of the beasts, they stampeded, about thirty of them, down the hill, towards me.

As swift as an arrow leaving a bow (a slight exaggeration, but allow me licence to colour the event), I jumped over the barbed-wire fence and into the coppice for safety. However, to my extreme horror, the rest of the herd were crashing through the woodland, trampling everything flat as they came.

Like the wind (excuse me, again), I raced through the coppice and towards the two horses which, to my great relief, scattered as I tore across the field between them. As if I now had wings, I flew over the hedge, the ditch, and stinging nettles in one bound and onto the road (that was real).

With smoke now billowing out from under the heels of my sandals (most likely plimsoles) and the tarmac melting beneath my feet, I shot along the road like a bolt of lightning. Within seconds, I was in the driveway, up the lane to the rear of the farmyard, and in an instant, I was standing once more at my grandfather's side.

I had such an amazing feeling of achievement and exhilaration. Not only had I escaped the bullocks and tamed the child-eating horses, but I was certain that I had broken all the world records of all the athletes that ever lived. Not bad for a ten-year-old!

My grandfather, however, took a very different view. Raising his arm, he took a swing at me with his walking stick, shouting at me to get back into the field and collect Nicky. I avoided the blow, which was extremely fortunate, stepped back and refused to obey his command. There was not a chance in hell that I was going back into that field, and as a result of my impudent stance, I became known from that moment on and forever after as the 'family coward,' a term that soon everyone learned.

I never knew about this title, but while chatting about the old times with Robbie a few years ago, he let it slip out, and on questioning my mother about it, she said, 'Oh yes, everyone knew that you were the family coward.'

Nobody ever asked me about the incident, probably because nobody in the family wanted to talk to me, bearing in mind who I was, but I do think that they were a little unjust. I always thought it odd that my brother, Lord of the Lies, was never subjected to such ridicule. Even at my grandfather's funeral years later, it was always, oh, John this and oh, John that, while I was left thinking that I must have had dog poo on my shoe.

The third summer, I was dumped there again. This time, even Nicky was seldom seen, and I spent most of the fortnight aimlessly wandering around. It seemed like even nature had gone on holiday. I was fed and barely spoken to unless it was a reprimand from my step-grandmother. But she always appeared to be busy, so I chose to keep out of her way as much as possible.

The one bright light was a pretty young American woman who lived with her US serviceman husband on the other side of the house. She was very pleasant, had a lovely smile, and I immediately fell in love with her. She obviously didn't know that I was the family coward and actually spoke to me without shouting. I counted out my pocket money and bought a large bar of chocolate from the post office at

Upper Dean, and I left it outside her door together with a love letter.

Normally, this kind of behaviour from a skinny little kid who had barely reached puberty would have been met with giggles or 'aww', but not so this time. The young woman's husband flew into a violently jealous rage and would have killed me if he could. It took days to quell his desire for my blood. His pretty wife had to look away from me whenever we passed, and my grandparents were not only furious, but worried stiff that they would have to find new tenants.

This was the final straw, and there was no chance of them ever having me stay at the Shelton Grange ever again.

10

My parents had found new friends who lived in a large house on Longley Road not far from Harrow on the Hill. The connection had been made through my brother and their son, both being in the same scout group.

Finding that the father of the lad was an ex-pilot and my father having been in the RAF for part of the war, there appeared to be some level of common ground between them.

Actually, my father had helped in the RAF motor pool at Stanmore during the war while the other chap had been flying in the skies over Europe, but my father didn't hold it against him, and they got along quite well.

Mr H impressed me with his ability to talk to other pilots on his huge, short-wave radio as the pilots flew their Spitfires over London. He even got one of them to talk to me, which was very exciting. He worked for the de Havilland Aircraft Company and took us out to their annual open day.

For some reason, it has always reminded me of 'The Fall and Rise of Reginald Perrin', a TV sitcom, and though I found most of it quite boring, I did go up in an aeroplane, a de Havilland Dove, even though I had to sit on a stranger's lap to do it.

As their friendship grew, the two couples started to go out for the evening together, and it was not long before I was to become a problem. My brother was not going to be home, not that he ever was, and therefore, there was no one to look after me. To help out, their son suggested that I should stay overnight with him at their house, and so it was agreed. I was only ten but he was fourteen and in the scouts with my brother, so he was safe company.

The young man and I played Ludo or fiddled about with the big radio, but eventually, it was time for bed. I was a little uneasy right from the start because it was a strange bed, and I had never shared a bed with anybody before, least of all a single bed.

We talked for a while, and he appeared to be interested in what I had to say. He then suggested that, because he wasn't really very tired, we should play a little game. It was dark and neither of us could see each other. He called the game 'What Is It' and explained how it should be played. In the game, I was to take his hand, place it on any part of my body, and he would have to guess what he was touching.

It sounded quite innocent to me, being only ten years old, and during the first few turns, it was, indeed, quite amusing. I put his hand on my nose, and he guessed that it was my ear. 'Wrong! Try again,' I chortled. It was that sort of game, and then it was his turn.

He put my hand on his elbow, and I guessed chin. What I noticed was that each time it came to be his turn, he would place my hand lower and lower, and it was not long before I guessed what he was trying to get me to do. I thought it was time for the game to stop.

'I'm going to sleep now!' I said, and quickly turned over.

I never told my parents about it, but I dreaded the idea of spending another night there and, fortunately, the occasion didn't present itself. After a short time, the family moved to Cheltenham, and I recall that my father received a telephone call from them and no further contact was made. I never knew what it was about, but there was a curious amount of bad temper involved.

This was the third time one of my brother's friends had been suspiciously friendly to me while I was still at primary school, and lo, two of them were scouts. I wondered if there was a badge available to stitch on to their green woollen jumpers called babysitter or even just touching scout.

It was a problem that, half the time, I was unaware of people's interest in me and intentions. Even when I was fifteen and Dave the Beard, whom I had met in the coffee bar in North Harrow, told me, 'You have such lovely eyes, just like a cow's', did I feel threatened.

Everybody liked him. He was a farmer and had a dairy herd on the other side of Harrow Hill. As far as I could see, he just had a passion for his cows and found them attractive. Nobody ever thought that he might have been gay. It didn't come into one's mind, and so, I was quite flattered.

Actually, cows really do have such lovely eyes. Those deep brown depths, however, do not mean that they are intelligent.

If they were, they surely would have joined the animal revolution and fought harder for their right to life.

11

As I approached my eleventh year, I developed an interest in early jazz, specifically early American Black jazz. I ventured out to buy my first 78rpm disc, and it turned out to be by a Black band recorded in 1928. To bore the uninitiated with detail, it was by King Oliver's Dixie Syncopators and the titles were 'Slow & Steady' and 'I'm Watching the Clock'.

This record was to be one of the first steps in my realisation that the world was not a very fair place, and that social injustice was rife and largely unaddressed in the good old US of A. Moreover, Black people were still being subjected to harsh discrimination, and white violence against them seemed totally uncontrolled.

On buying my second disc by Johnny Dodds, a part-Black, part-Cherokee clarinettist, matters were made worse when I then discovered the sad truth of the decimation of Native Americans, mostly at the hands of whites. I had always felt that the 'redskins' in films were given a hard time, and I started to read some of the accounts of the slaughter of these people at the hands of the US army. This, in combination with my flirtation with the young lady at Shelton

Grange and her husband's extreme reaction, seriously dete-
riorated the status of the United States in my mind.

I was living quite close to the USAF base at Northolt, and
it had been noted locally that the behaviour of some of the
servicemen could have been improved, especially when alcohol and perhaps a Buick V8 got together. Needless to say,
I began to question why they were being given so much ac-
colade.

The Korean War had fairly recently ended, and though,
as a child, I had no comprehension of its cause or its casualties, I had been curiously affected by the squadrons of B52
bombers and Dakota transports that flew overhead, day after day. One could hear the drone of the bombers long before their actual appearance. Their numbers were countless
and the skies dark from their silhouettes. Nobody I knew
seemed to give it a thought, but it all seemed too ominous
to be forgotten.

I couldn't begin to imagine the quantity of bombs that
these monstrous denizens dropped on North Korea, and the
number of innocent people turned to dust must have been
devastating. Only a few years had passed since the end of
the Second World War, and yet the Americans and British
seemed totally unphased by the previous war despite our
own economic plight, indulging in a bloodletting on the
other side of the world for a reason that only political fantasy can justify. How could they protect Democracy when
they barely understood what it actually was?

A couple of years later, I had a dream, obviously influenced by these squadrons flying overhead, the memory of

which has not left me. It was a dark stormy night in the dream, and among the broken clouds, I glimpsed the same ominous squadrons flying high in the sky in a triangular formation. Gradually, they circled round, lower and lower, until they were directly overhead.

As each wave came down, they crashed into the street in front of me but no longer as aircraft. They had become locusts, which turned to mush as more and more piled on top of each other. I could see it all in the light of the streetlamps as they were washed away by a torrential rain that swept down between the houses. It was not a terribly frightening dream, but the spectacle had certainly made an impression on me.

Something that I didn't know until very recently was that during the Second World War, B-52 bombers were flown low by RAF Lancasters, a manoeuvre used to take the flak. Many Lancasters and their crews were lost as a result.

Later, there were other aircraft in the skies around my home on Albert Road, but this time, they were English as opposed to American. It was exhilarating to see a vast, triangular Vulcan bomber cruising just above the chimneys, or pairs of Canberras and Meteors circling in the sunny summer sky. Seeing and hearing the loud boom of the ill-fated DH-110 going through the sound barrier before disappearing as a tiny speck into the blue was an unforgettable sight. However, none of these planes seemed to have the same deadly, remorseless purpose as the B-52s but were more the spectacle of a great engineering feat.

At night, all was silent except for the distant metallic *pan... pan... pan* of the goods trains shunting back and forth at Wealdstone's goods yard, muffled only during the winter months by the occasional stinking, sulphurous fog that choked out the light from the old gas streetlamps.

It was all a million miles away from the southern states and the old Wild, Wild West. Far from the Black bodies swinging in the southern breeze and tepees burning on the old Cheyenne trails.

12

Nower Hill on the outskirts of Pinner was always a place of interest. It was the wooded section of an agricultural belt which stretched from North Harrow to Hatch End, bordered on the north by Pinner and on the south by Headstone Lane.

It was there that three of us—Teddy and Mickey, both eleven years old, and I, one year younger—fell afoul of two young men with air rifles. The first thing we heard was the crack of the airguns and the rattle of the pellets cascading through the leaves. There they were, two twenty-year-old morons pointing their rifles at us.

Initially, the intimidation was verbal. They had stripped a couple of hazel switches from the surrounding bushes, and forcing Teddy to the ground, started to lash him unmercifully. Then it was Mickey's turn, and then inevitably mine—or so I expected.

It was probably my seemingly emaciated state that prohibited them from whipping me. Thinking about it, they may have thought that my skin might fall off or that my bones might have jutted out of my body if they lashed me just a little too hard. Or maybe they thought that I would just fall onto the ground like a pile of spilled minced offal. Whatever the reason, I remained untouched.

After more verbal abuse, they told us to run, taking pot shots at us as we fled.

On the way home, the three of us decided that we would never say a word about it in case those two bastards were to track us down and do even worse things to us.

Once again, that Fair Maid of Chance entered the story and uncovered the secret of the day's events. It was all there, as if written in blood for everyone to see, right on Teddy's buttocks.

It was Teddy's mother who saw them first while he was taking a bath later that evening. Gathering him up in a towel, she came down to where I lived to verify Teddy's story.

'Is it true that my son came by the red stripes on his rump at the hands of two young men?'

Off they went to the police station in Wealdstone to report the attack and where Teddy had to display his bottom once again. Whether or not it was photographed, I can only conjecture, but it would have been an ideal companion to the bounty photo of the grey squirrel on the police station notice board: 'A shilling paid for every grey squirrel tail.'

It took a long while, but eventually, the two were arrested. By this time, having failed the eleven plus as I said before, I was at a secondary modern school, pompously designated Headstone County Secondary Modern School.

My form teacher was a female demon who we all knew as Mrs Robbins, which was probably a pseudonym to cover her dark incarnation. The class tolerated her taunts that 'none of you will ever compare with my handsome and beloved son.'

The Maid of Chance had still not let go of her grip on the hazel switching event, though much time had passed, and she once again intervened.

It was eighteen months later when Mrs Robbins' wonderful son, one of the two who had attacked us, was sentenced to serve a period of time in prison. I can't remember for how long, but the good thing was that the evil woman was so distraught and felt so disgraced, that she resigned her post and was never to be seen again.

Other things that happened at Nower Hill were less intensive but quite interesting, such as being chased by a rather frisky cow, finding a war-time scout car hidden in a derelict garage (us kids all thought it was a German one), or watching chafer grubs falling out of a rotten tree. There were tall electricity pylons which carried the magic Danger of Death notices if one climbed more than a few feet, and there was a place where one could go tobogganing when it snowed.

A few years later, when I was fifteen, it was on the four-mile route from my home to the Queen's Head public house in Pinner where rough cider was five pence for half a pint, and ordinary bitter was seven pence. How quickly things changed!

13

Headstone Secondary Modern was a great place—if you were a boy with a masochistic inclination. I can't speak for the girls there, but there were times when, as an eleven-year-old, I would ask myself, *What have I done wrong to end up here?*

I must have been one of the few children to have failed the eleven plus at Pinner Park Juniors that year because there were only a handful of kids in my group that I knew. I was pleased to form a stronger relationship with a boy in the second year who had, at one time, lived on my road.

Peter was fairly unstable in certain ways, most of which I was unaware of but became more obvious as time passed. It was his influence, or should I say intervention, that saved me from the obligatory duck under the drinking fountain that every boy in the new intake had to suffer. This degradation was at the hands of the notorious school bullies, Barney Becket and Barry Dodds. The price I paid was only to have the top of my hair vigorously rubbed by their grubby, wet hands, a much better deal than having to sit in class with a wet collar and a bruised face.

There were three people to fear at the school: the headmaster, Manson, who was overly fond of the cane, and the nefarious duo, Dodds and Becket.

Of the three, Becket was probably the most dangerous. His eyes had that cold, calculating stare, lids slightly hooded, like those of a cat about to attack an enemy. His moves and moods were unpredictable, and his appearance in the playground was always disturbing, like a cold, sharp gust of wind on a warm, sunny day. His close ally, Barry Dodds, was a little taller and facially less threatening, but as a unit, they were a nightmare. They always attacked as a pair, usually with a devastating effect.

Manson was a cross between an SS officer and a pit bull, and it was best to keep out of his way. From his appearance, I deduced he was German and couldn't understand how he became a headmaster of an English school so soon after the war. In fact, he was there in 1943 which, I suppose, makes it even worse. But of course, he wasn't really a German. It was just that he liked to behave like an SS guard.

If a child got three detentions during the course of a week, which was easy to achieve, it would automatically become a caning offence. The punishment would be six strokes of the cane delivered by the delighted Mr Manson, and it was probably only his blood pressure that stopped him from indulging himself more fully in this, his favourite pastime.

In the mid-1950s, class sizes often reached fifty children plus. Classroom sizes were not adequate for these vast numbers, and class exams were virtually impossible to run efficiently. In the spring term of my first year, we all sat the class examination. Each pupil sat so close to their neighbour, it was impossible not to see what the other had written.

Some clever, dispassionate teacher noticed, while marking the papers, that many carried the same errors and/or details, which suggested to his sleuth-like mind that many of us had been copying from each other. Manson, on hearing the good news, oiled his canes, ready for action, and called on the honesty of the cheats to declare themselves.

One by one, our hands went up. It seemed like most had been unable to keep their eyes glued to their own papers. All those who had cheated were to be caned and were sent by their respective teachers to stand outside Manson's door.

The queue grew and grew, all of them having admitted their crime. Eventually, the corridor could take no more. When Manson opened his door with his usual aggression, his face dropped. He quickly calculated the hundreds of strokes that he would have to administer, and slowly, he slunk back into his office in dismay. We didn't hear another word about it, but never again did we sit exams in such overcrowded conditions.

School dinners at Headstone were just as bad as those at primary school, but colder. We were assured that we would be given the same food as the teachers. So when cabbage was served, why did the teachers have green pieces on their plates while the children just had stalks? To make matters worse, the canteen was a Nissen hut at the top end of the playing field and so small that only about thirty could eat in it at any one time. Therefore, everybody had to queue outside until a seat was vacant. It wasn't so bad in the summer, but winter rain, snow and frost certainly made it into something of an ordeal.

Teaching methods were almost as bad as the food with a few exceptions, notably English. Mr Wilkinson (I believe that was his name) was superb. He was enthusiastic about his subject matter and infused that spirit onto his students. The way he taught not only raised our understanding of the language of literature but also encouraged us to absorb history and geography simultaneously.

Two of the others, the French and maths teachers, were different. In both cases, they asked the class at the start of the year who had done the subject before and exactly how far they had gone. For most of us, French was a foreign language, but so were geometry and algebra. There were always a couple of bright sparks who had advanced further than the others, and those two teachers told us that we would have to catch up with the leaders without any tuition.

Thus, for the two years that I stayed at Headstone, my comprehension of the two subjects remained behind the point from where the classes had first started. Compulsory detentions followed, and I received two each week. I was doubly careful not to get a third for fear of Manson's cane.

The aforementioned Mrs Robbins exerted her authority by ensuring that we all had three hours of homework each night and six at the weekend. Faked homework books became the order of the day with carefully forged parental signatures at the foot of each page.

On one occasion, a girl suffering from a fairly severe stomach upset, asked to go to the loo. Permission was refused. The girl's pleading went unheeded, and her tears were met with no compassion. Slowly, a puddle of diarrhoea formed beneath her seat and continued to drip from the back of her chair for some minutes.

Her frock was saturated, but the hard-as-stone Mrs Robbins took no notice of her plight except to admonish her for her lack of self-control. The lesson continued, and the girl had to stay seated. Despite the health implications, we all had to remain in the classroom until the end of the session.

In April of that first year, 1955, the class went to the swimming pool at Harrow outdoor baths to learn how to swim. The snow still lingered on the grass and ice covered a large section of the deep end. Unfazed by the cold, the PT teacher told us to change into our swimming gear and get into the water. We stood there freezing and shivering in the shallow end as our coach cajoled us into submerging our shoulders under the water because it was warmer. The water temperature was forty-one degrees Fahrenheit.

Slowly and involuntarily, I started to fold until my torso was horizontal to the water and my face firmly implanted in it. I was lifted out in the same position, vigorously towelled down until I could straighten out, and the lesson was called to a halt. 'Belsen Barry's' lack of fat had saved the day once more, though it did take some time for me to get warm again.

During the second year I spent at Headstone, life seemed to be a little less fraught. The food was the same, but Manson was less visible. However, two incidents took place which were both shocking and bizarre.

We had a new music teacher who seemed quite dedicated to his subject. He was, I suppose, a little effeminate, with somewhat delicate features and a slender build. A rumour started to circulate that he was 'not quite right' and that 'the boys had better watch out'. One cloudy morning, while he was on playground duty, the mob moved in.

The first assault came in a hail of crab apples along with a lot of shouting. That was followed by a full assault from a group of boys, who then forced him to the ground and proceeded to beat him. Other teachers arrived and managed to rescue the hapless individual from the onslaught and carried him inside the school building while a throng of pupils hurled a tirade of verbal abuse.

That was the last time we saw him. The strange thing is that I don't recall anybody getting into trouble for the attack, and one got the feeling that violence of one sort or another could flourish unchecked in the school.

The second incident took place during the summer term, fortunately my last at Headstone. Walking from one lesson to another between the cluster of prefabricated classrooms, we were confronted firstly, by a double window hanging crookedly against the exterior cladding of one of the huts. Then around the corner of the building, we were met with a door, once the entrance to the classroom, lying flat on the tarmac at the bottom of a short flight of steps.

There had been a religious instruction lesson given by a fairly well-built and bespectacled teacher. The students included Dodds and Becket, the infamous bullying duo. Sometime during the lesson, these two arose and attacked him with their chairs, overturning desks and creating general havoc in the classroom. The teacher, in self-defence and probably shocking the demonic duo beyond their belief, hurled one boy through the window and the other through the door. Both the door and window had been shut. That was the end of their school days because I didn't see them around the school anymore.

At last, the problem of the maths detentions was finally solved during the second half of my second year. I had met another boy in the park, two years older than I, on the way back from school. What was incomprehensible to me was simplicity itself to him, and so it was that he did most of my maths homework for me and, the same time, explained the things that my teacher had failed to do.

To exert some control over the pupils, it was announced that we all had to wear our school uniforms on weekends, even if we were out with our parents. Any child seen by a member of staff outside the school without a uniform would get a detention. The excuse for this edict was to promote the honour of the school. Fortunately, no one took it seriously, neither the edict nor the honour, and treated it with the disregard it deserved. Whoever dreamed up this absurdity had obviously lost the plot, but I suppose many of the staff had already reached that stage. The fact that they continued to try to teach at Headstone was the proof.

I had taken the thirteen-plus examination in desperation to get out of that pit of despondency and had miraculously passed. That July, my sojourn at Headstone Secondary Modern came to an end. I inhaled a long, deep breath of relief as I went through the gates for the very last time.

14

It was during my eleventh year that I started to smoke. It began with the occasional puff of somebody else's fag and pinching the odd one from my mother. But when my pocket money was raised to two shillings a week, I could then buy five Woodbines for eleven old pence.

To buy more, I had to be resourceful. For example, the price of a haircut was between two shillings and half a crown, but I found a place near Wealdstone where I could get a haircut for a shilling by an aged ex-army barber known locally as 'the blind barber'. The temptation to save half my haircut money to enable me to buy more cigarettes over-ruled my misgivings about his reputation, so I plucked up the courage and entered the shop. He was a nice old man, cheery and friendly, and he was positively welcoming.

His visual problem was only moderate in my estimation. As I sat down in the chair, he inquired how I wanted my hair to be cut. I replied that I didn't want it to be cut too short, to which he replied, 'Pardon, could you speak up a little, young man. I'm a bit hard of hearing.'

So I responded with a half shouted, 'Not too short, please!'

He, in turn, called out, 'Just tell me when to stop.'

All went fine for the first five minutes, he snipping and chattering away about the weather and the local news, but now we were getting to the crucial part, and it was necessary for me to study the progress more carefully.

'I think that's enough now, thanks,' I said.

He responded, 'Is that enough off yet?'

'Yes, thanks.'

'Okay,' he said and carried on cutting.

A few more minutes passed, and I again said, 'That's enough, thanks!' more loudly.

'Fine, just a bit more, you say,' and he carried on, with my hair and I visibly disappearing into the chair.

At last, he said, 'I won't take any more off; otherwise, you might look like you've just come out of the army.'

The fact was that I looked more like I had just come out of my father's wallet. I had a very distinct case of moth with various sections of my scalp quite visible where no vestige of hair remained, and the rest of my head with only a millimetre or two of hair left.

He held up a mirror behind me so that I could admire myself.

'How's that, son?' he asked.

I paid him the shilling and left the shop. I shall not comment on the combination of deafness and problematic eyesight in the profession of haircutting but can only say that a study of this phenomenon could be quite interesting.

At the post office next door, I bought a packet of five Player's Weights and a box of matches 'for my dad' and scurried away to find a dark hole in which to hide until night-fall, hoping that in those few hours, my hair might grow a centimetre or two. I had smoked all five cigarettes within the hour as I tried to conjure up a story as to how my head had ended up in such a state. Nothing but the truth came to mind, and as my mother said on my return, 'Well, I don't suppose you'll be going there again!'

During the summer holidays, I spent a lot of time at Harrow outdoor swimming baths, and although I have never been able to swim any great distance, with my bones having a tendency to sink, I found the exercise invigorating despite the forty-minute walk there and back. In the beginning, I would never go into the deep end, but by necessity, I had to pass along it on one occasion.

A young girl a couple of years older than I, and whose name I later found out was Beryl, ran at me, giving me a hefty shove towards the water. Under normal circumstances, I would have splashed around and got to the edge without too much of a fuss, but unfortunately, as I skidded into the pool, feet first, my head struck the side and knocked me senseless for several seconds. When I came to, I realised that I was sinking, and I made a desperate lunge for the surface.

As I came up, in my anxiety, I gasped for air before I reached the surface. It was much too soon, and I sucked into my lungs a large quantity of chlorinated liquid. As I sank once again, I felt a calm, warm sensation creeping through my body. I could see my hand outstretched above me through the sunlit water in a kind of disconnected vision as I continued to sink.

When I was all but unconscious, somebody grasped my hand and hauled me out. The lifeguard was called over to officiate. Finding me alive, he started to berate me for being in the deep end when I couldn't swim. If ever someone needed to be struck from behind with a large wet fish, I think it was he.

I met Beryl a couple of weeks later and thought she was lovely. I wondered what it might be like to swim in her beauty. As an experience, I can say that I was glad to have had it. I have a theory that in times of great stress, the brain offers a way-out option, a sort of gentle release system.

I believe I started to smoke to make me appear less of a pushover. Being a good runner showed that I obviously had some strength, but my bony little frame precluded a lot of my peers from taking me seriously. So smoke I did.

I also collected matchbox labels. They were informative, artistic, and cultural. Some match labels, particularly Indian ones, seemed to have the whole of Indian culture on display, from maidens on swings to religious icons, but the problem was, and probably still is, that they were worthless. If ever you saw a boy with one foot in the gutter and the other on the kerb, you would know that he was either looking for matchboxes or dog ends. If it turned out that he was looking for both, then that was me.

I had resurrected my father's old cigarette rolling machine, and foul as it was, I indulged in an early form of recycling, you might say. A few years ago, nearly fifty years after I had ceased to walk in the gutter, I put my collection of about two thousand match labels into a local auction where somebody boldly bid twelve pounds. I shouldn't think the price paid would have covered the cost of the shoe leather I used in their acquisition.

Amongst them were Victorian labels with diagrams of how to light a match, First World War ones overprinted with 'Waste Not, Want Not', and Second World War ones with 'Save Fuel'. Others documented various aspects of social and political history, from Sputniks to Colorado Beetles, but for all that, were apparently valueless.

There were two types of matches: the safety type which needed to be struck on the side of the box and the phosphorous strike-anywhere type.

My friendship with Peter had continued for a couple of years, and though there were a lot of bad things going on with him, I became complacently drawn into his iniquity. This eventually came to an abrupt halt when he struck a match of the second type, and while the phosphorous was still burning, he stuck it on my lip, causing a burn that wept for three weeks.

I was already losing my nerve with the knife games that had suddenly become popular with the kids in the park. The idea of having a knife going through my foot or through my hand didn't appear to be a useful prospect, and considering Peter's apparent lack of self-control, I began to distance myself from him. I shut the door finally on our amity when he suggested that I should offer my services to a ballroom/dance-hall owner for five pounds a time, for which he would get paid a fiver for the introduction.

'No thanks, Peter. I don't think so!'

Two years later, he was arrested for leading a gang of local youngsters in a number of local burglaries, and soon after that, his family moved off to Australia.

Northolt USAF base played host during the 1950s to a travelling fairground. I never quite understood how the word 'fair' became part of the term, these places being a hotbed of unfairness, what with their rifles having off-true barrels and so on.

The distance from Albert Road was about six or seven miles and only took half an hour on my bike.

I arrived at about 11am, only to find that hardly any of the stalls were up and running. Finding one with the shutters open, I thought I might squander a few minutes by trying my skill at rolling my few pennies onto a board, then into the pocket of the large lady behind the counter. The idea was that I would place a penny at the top of a little wooden chute and hope that it would settle exactly over one of the circles on the board which formed the countertop. Prizes ranged from getting your penny back—or better still, two—up to a goldfish or, at the top, a canary in a cage. Disgusting really, but in those days, respect for these creatures was not on the agenda.

So I rolled a penny and lost, then another, and lost. On the third try, the penny circled a couple of times before settling exactly over a top prize circle.

'Look!' I yelled. 'I've won!'

The big lady leaned forward, dropping fag ash on the board.

'Oh, what a shame, dearie. It's not quite on,' she said as she gently tapped the coin off centre with her middle finger. 'Not quite on.'

Disillusioned, I turned away. There were no witnesses, and there was nothing I could say. I was actually dumbfounded. I didn't know that adults could be such cheats, least of all big, mummy ones.

'Bye, dearie,' she called as I got back on my bike.

What would I have done with a damned canary, anyway?

Every winter, and often during the rest of the year, I would get tonsillitis. This went on from the age of ten until they were finally removed when I was eighteen. Smoking did not help the situation, but the infections were already happening before I started that unpleasant habit.

The woman who lived in the flat upstairs, Mrs Marshall, had said to my mother when I was about six years old, 'Barry is becoming nasal. You should do something about it.'

My mother, taking it as a personal insult, rushed me off to the doctor, who said, 'Ah, adenoids!' So my parents took me to hospital, sneaked quietly away without saying goodbye, and only returned when it was time to collect me several days later.

Normally, tonsils and adenoids were removed together, but Dr Lucy Parker, our doctor, thought that my tonsils were fine. Well, they were until I had my adenoids removed, and then they weren't.

I coughed and coughed my way through childhood and through my teens and, at one point, ended up at a TB clinic. Fortunately, I didn't have TB, but I did have tonsillitis, which Dr Parker treated with penicillin. When she eventually retired several years later, her daughter-in-law took over the practice with her husband.

Taking a look at the offending objects one day, she said, 'Oh dear, why on earth have you still got those?' She explained that it was a little risky to remove them after puberty with possible complications, such as death or becoming a contralto. But she also said, with a smile I might add, 'But some people have been known to survive.'

We joked about it, and I thought I'd rather be a singer than a cougher, so the job was done. I am not dead; I am not a contralto—shame, really. I could have made some money there—and I don't cough much, mostly when I'm eating toast.

I wondered, Was I or was I not becoming nasal or was it that I just liked to whine a lot. On the other hand, was it just a fickle piece of criticism thrown in to upset my mother? I guess I'll never know.

Odd things did happen! At the time, I put it down to spring fever or the passage through puberty because I couldn't explain it otherwise. In our lounge, to the side of the French windows, was a dining chair, and on a bright, sunny morning in early spring, I was compelled to sit on this seat with my back to the light. When I say compelled, it was not that I was forced to sit there but rather drawn into its embrace by some strange magnetism.

Slowly, I felt myself ebb away, my breathing becoming shallow, and I lost all vitality. I felt myself drifting into the air, and eventually, I hovered over the kitchen door looking down on myself, slumped in the dining chair. I sat quite still, seemingly asleep. I floated down and back to the seat by the window and regained myself.

It was a bit odd looking at myself, not the sort of thing that happens every day. A few days later, the same thing happened, but this time, it wasn't quite like it was before. I was drawn to the chair and hovered once more over the door, but the boy sitting there seemed more distant, colder, vaguer.

I could feel that something else was present around him and that it became necessary for me to return. But there was the problem. I could not immediately find the route back, and I could see the boy visibly fading away as I watched. My return was being blocked. The episode passed, but I felt quite weak and tired for an hour or two afterwards.

The chair did entice me on a few other occasions, but I managed to avoid the call, and for years after, I often looked at that particular spot with apprehension. The odd thing about it all was the initial feeling of total peace, which was quite appealing. Following that, in the same year, I had a couple of blackouts at school, which were a bit unnerving but, thankfully, got me out of assembly.

On both occasions, it was the spring sun shining behind me which seemed to be the trigger. Without warning, everything went black, and I felt as if I was going to be sick. Bearing in mind that I could not see, having blacked out, I miraculously found my way out of the assembly hall, down a long flight of stairs, along a corridor, and up another couple of steps into the boys' washroom. I was sure that I couldn't have done this blindly without falling over or bumping into something. So what happened?

It was the same on both occasions, and nobody mentioned that I had acted strangely or asked me if I was all right. The events passed, and I felt perfectly okay except for a mild headache. Otherwise, drifting through puberty posed no problems: no croaky voice, no vigorously sprouting hair out of my ears, just a few rather aggravating pustules around my face, and that was it. I was no longer a child… well, only physically.

15

It seems to me that bigger people always want to make one's life difficult unless one has lots of money, which I didn't. In July 1955, my brother reached the grand old age of fifteen, and to celebrate the event, he was to hold a party at our flat. My parents had arranged to be out until the early hours so that he could have a good time without their intrusive presence. The only problem was me, which they had overlooked.

Having seen him help himself to my mother's cigarettes, I totally underestimated what a terrible thing it would be if I were to take one of his. He had left nearly full packet of Camel cigarettes on the windowsill and had gone out. This, in itself, should have rung some kind of alarm in my mind, but unfortunately, it didn't.

I examined the packet closely and felt sure that he would not miss just one, especially since I had carefully rearranged them so they would appear untouched. Little did I know then that this was a carefully laid trap that he had devised to get me out of the way when his friends arrived later that evening.

As soon as they had all arrived a little after seven o'clock, he dragged me in front of them in a show of feigned anger and accused me of stealing one of his cigarettes. Without giving me a chance to confirm or deny the accusation (it was at this point irrelevant, even if I had not taken one), he hit me across the face, threw me out of the flat, and locked the door behind me.

The party broke up at about 11pm, and when everyone had left, he pulled me back indoors and ordered me to go to bed. I was not surprised that he could keep up this show of anger for so long, and I refused. In retaliation for my disobedience, he refused to let me go to bed, a big problem when having to share your bedroom with a bully. I settled down under a couple of damp towels on the settee and went off to sleep.

My parents returned at around 3am and were surprised to find me curled up in the lounge. I explained what had happened, and all seemed calm at first, but as the warm air buffeted against the cold, lightning flashed across my mother's face, and the tirade commenced.

In the end, she insisted that, in the future, I obey my brother in whatever way he demanded; otherwise, there would be real trouble. I was then pushed off to bed. She had just given my brother, who stood smirking behind her, carte blanche to bully me in any way he chose. Never again did I take a cigarette from my brother, despite his habit of helping himself to anything he wanted of mine.

The following spring, during one of our regular fights, I managed to surprise him. His regular and favourite ploy was to get me on the ground from behind, put his legs around my waist, and crush the breath out of me. His legs were quite powerful from all the cycle racing he did, but for me, it was quite an ordeal.

He had misjudged the angle this time, and I managed to get my arm around his head. As he squeezed my middle, I squeezed his head in return. Furiously, he tried to extricate himself, but I increased the pressure to the utmost of my strength. I could see the skin under his left eye begin to tear, and a flap about two inches long hung down over his cheek.

A truce was called. He snipped off the flap with a pair of scissors and wanted desperately to give me what for. But I refused and boasted that I had won and that if we started again, I would have to do the same to his other eye.

My mother intervened for the only time I can remember and told us to 'call it a day'. That was our last physical fight for several years and successfully put an end to him physically bullying me. There was just one occasion which I actually instigated and showed him just how weak he was—a sort of payback, one might say.

In that same year, I fell in love with a shirt I had seen in a shop window in Wealdstone. The shop was a dingy little hutch on the bridge over the railway lines. But for all the grime from the steam trains passing underneath and the traffic passing over the bridge, the shirt still retained its beautiful carmine-red tint. It was just a little faded from the sun, having been in the window for so long. A fine line of black stitching edged the collar and cuffs in the style of a proper teddy-boy shirt. I just had to have it.

I saved all my pocket money for a couple of months, checking each weekend that it was still there. Finally, when I had all the money ready, I rushed to the shop and bought it. The collar was a little too large, but it didn't matter ...the shirt was mine, all mine!

When I got home and excitedly showed it to my mother, I could tell that she was not pleased. Within a couple of weeks, it vanished from my drawer and was never seen again.

That shirt was the first of my clothes to disappear. Sometimes they were later seen on a relative or, worse still, in a stinking heap on the floor of one of my brother's friends. My mother was determined to be the one who bought my clothes and, as such, felt that she had the right to dispose of them whenever she wanted.

Her favourite thing to do was to tog me out, which she did once a year when she received an annual bonus from Kodak. This often worked to my advantage because, not only did I get a new school uniform, shorts, and trousers, but she felt it necessary to use my brother as a role model in dressing me up. Not finding quite the right stuff, and my being a lot smaller than my brother, I found that I was then able to manipulate her into buying me clothes that were more to my taste.

My mother loved to go shopping, or should I say spending, but what she loved most was the attention. I remember one Saturday afternoon, not long before Christmas 1955, she left my father and me outside a dress shop on College Road, Harrow. It was very cold and wet standing there while she tried on six dresses. The performance took something over an hour, during which time she expected the shop assistant to fawn over her all the while.

The assistant's undivided attention ceased after half an hour, the poor girl showing signs of fatigue. Failing to zealously enthuse about how beautiful my mother looked in this dress or that, my mother began to become irritable. This inevitably led to my mother breaking down in tears. Coming out of the shop without a new dress and on the point of screaming, slamming the door behind her, she howled that she had never been treated so rudely, ad infinitum.

As more money flowed into the house, these outings became more frequent, and her misery grew noticeably. At home, I tried to keep out of the firing line, but the flat was too small. Shopkeepers of all types were likely targets, and had they known how volatile my mother was, they would have done well to shut up shop and start again elsewhere.

On one occasion, on her way back from Kodak, she called into the local grocers at the Quadrant down Harrow View. The shopkeeper had been suffering a serious family crisis of some sort and was obviously not in the position to be his usual jolly self. On entering the shop, my mother greeted him with her usual flirty entrée, 'How's my favourite boyfriend today?'

The unexpected response of, 'Not today, Joan, not today' nearly knocked her over backwards. She blustered out of the shop, and arriving home a few minutes later, she almost blew herself apart with rage.

'How dare he! Who does he think he is! Do you know what he said? He said, "Not today, Joan, not today". I'm not going in that bloody shop again to be insulted like that!' and on and on. As a result, she prohibited the family from buying groceries there ever again, even if it meant catching a bus to North Harrow to get a bottle of milk. The shop closed its doors for several months, not that it had anything to do with my mother's outburst. It was more likely a serious health issue in the shopkeeper's family.

Eventually, there was hardly a shop at the Quadrant whose owner didn't quake on her approach. Deep down, I think she knew it because it seemed like I was spending more time doing the local fetching and carrying than before. She was always pleased when a shop changed hands. It meant that there was somebody new with whom she could flirt.

I recall, with not a little amusement, an occasion when I was returning from the Quadrant with eleven pounds of potatoes in a string bag that I had suspended from the handlebars of my bike. As I pedalled along, my centre of gravity moved slowly to one side as the bag moved away from the centre of the bars. At the same time, a concrete lamp standard that had only been recently erected, was looming ahead.

As I drew level with it, the potato bag emptied its contents onto the road. If that wasn't funny enough, my attention was diverted for a split second, causing my face and the lamppost to collide. I am not sure which of us was to blame, but for several months, I eyed the lamp base with suspicion and felt sure that, in that instant, it had leaned over to give me a black eye.

Apart from the shopping, I used to clean the flat each Saturday morning in a vain attempt to justify my eating and sleeping there, and unlike my brother, I found it impossible to get a Saturday job. I admit that he never had a problem finding one kind of income or another, and indeed, some of them appeared to be quite legitimate.

Whereas most Saturday jobs would be passed on to family or friends when the current employee moved on, it was something that never quite happened in my case and was due, on at least one occasion, to my brother's bad behaviour.

One day, he had told me that he was going to give up his florist delivery job that Friday. Seeing the opportunity to fill the vacancy, I telephoned the shopkeeper immediately to offer my services.

She was appalled at my nerve. Having sacked him three months previously for a serious misdemeanour, she certainly wasn't going to entertain the idea of employing another member of his family, even if the sky fell in. He was lucky that she hadn't called the police, she added.

So where did he get his money? He was certainly never short of it.

I was met with a similar refusal from the milkman. My brother had given up the job on a Saturday, and I agreed with the man to take over the following Monday morning, a school holiday. All I had to do was go to the milkman's shop at three o'clock sharp on the Sunday afternoon to learn what as expected of me.

I kept the appointment only to find the shop closed, and on the Monday morning, another youngster was doing the promised job. The milkman gave neither an explanation nor apology. Personally, I would have changed our milkman, but not knowing why he had so suddenly changed his mind clouded the issue.

Other attempts at finding work were to no avail. Dragging myself around every shop in North Harrow, Harrow, and Wealdstone, with the exception of women's clothing shops, was like the labours of Hercules. I did this week after week, only to return home and be accused of not trying hard enough. I think the problem was I looked too thin and frail. It would not have been surprising. I'm sure that I got shorter and grubbier from fatigue each weekend so that by the end of each trek, I probably resembled an old cat with mange.

On 31st December 1957, my mother and I stayed up for the ringing in of the new year, as if waiting for it would bring some life-changing event, which in a way it did.

My father had gone away on a job for Walter Kidde and was not due back for a couple of days. My brother had left England to hitchhike around the world. The fact that he was shacked up with a wealthy Frenchman in Paris at the time hinted at a different type of hitching.

My mother obviously felt neglected, and my meagre company was not sufficient for her to take her mind off the

lack of party spirit. It could have been the perfect opportunity for her to sparkle in a new dress and earrings, get
slightly drunk, and possibly insult somebody, not purposefully for she was never able to keep her thoughts to herself.

At about five minutes to midnight, she finally lost her
grip and thought that I would make a good target for vent-
ing her frustration. As she raged through the magic hour,
she eventually declared, 'You will never be half the man that
your brother is!' In a way, it was a relief, but it also meant
that I was valued at less than half of nothing, which was a
little difficult to swallow at the age of thirteen.

So I did what any child would do and disappeared into
the park for the next three hours, walking around and trying to think where I could live and who would be kind
enough to treat me like a person. At that time of night, the
thought of banging on somebody's door and asking, 'Can I
come and live with you?' did not seem like a good idea.

Feeling rather cold, I couldn't think of anywhere I could
shelter and keep warm until the morning. So I dragged myself back to the flat and crept off to bed. My mother had already gone to bed and obviously knew that I would be back,
leaving the kitchen door unlocked for my return.

Nothing was mentioned about it again, and she seemed
to have forgotten the incident. I often looked at my friends'
mothers with a kind of longing when they were being nice
to their children. I would have loved to hear the words,
'Would you like to come here and live with us?' But unfortunately, it never happened.

My father returned a couple of days later, and after about

ten days, my brother turned up saying that he had run out of money. He had been away for approximately three weeks, and I thought that hitchhiking around the world was one thing, but doing it the week before Christmas was another.

It was doomed to fail unless there had been a plan B, that being the wealthy, fur-coat-clad, new Citroen-DS-driving, Parisian, flat-owning man whose existence was now denied. Anyway, he got his hero's welcome, and my mother was glad to have her boy back.

16

During the summer holiday period between leaving Headstone and going to Kilburn Polytechnic, I continued to meet with my maths homework mentor. He was a fee-paying pupil at John Lyon School in Harrow, just down the road from the famous public school, and was obviously from a different social background than I.

Dan played the alto saxophone and had a liking for jazz. His favourite was Earl Bostic, whose tune, 'Flamingo', was a big hit in the fifties. It made a change not to be ridiculed for liking 1920s jazz.

Within a few days, he introduced me to his fellow John Lyon boys, most of whom were not opposed to the music either. At age thirteen, I was a few years younger than many of them, and I became a kind of mascot.

They were a bit of a wild bunch and were not shy about having a good time, but they also had a predilection for gambling with cards. I had already lost many a good halfpenny in the park, playing card games like Pontoon, Brag, and Poker until dark. Having so little to lose, it was a source of cheap amusement.

One afternoon, a group of us started to play Pontoon at Dan's house. The stakes were low with a sixpenny limit, which was more than I could afford. As the game was governed by both chance and luck, it fell to me after a while to take the bank.

Among the group was one Martin J., who suddenly demanded that the limit should be raised to two shillings. The rest of the players withdrew, not wanting to get that involved. I had no choice as I was the bank and couldn't back out.

On his first hand, Martin drew an ace and a king, then a jack, queen, ace, and for the next thirteen consecutive hands, he drew twenty-ones in varying combinations. Despite my asking to leave the game after my initial losses, I was suddenly in debt for thirty shillings. Having only two shillings a week pocket money at that time, I was in serious trouble.

Martin was not to be thwarted and demanded that I pay him by the weekend. He wasn't interested in any excuses and became very aggressive. He was eventually taken aside by the others to quiet him down. I don't know what was said, but the event was quite disturbing and had the effect of curbing any future desire to gamble. There were plenty of other ways to lose money. After all, it's less traumatic to stand over a drain with holes in one's pockets.

I was certain that the cards were not marked, so I couldn't explain how he managed to consistently win for a total of fifteen consecutive hands. A year later, Martin became a persona non grata when it was learned that he had

been beating up his girlfriend, and that was the last I knew
of Martin J.

It was during that summer of 1957, when we all went
round to Martin's house in Headstone Lane, that I was sent
on an errand on my bike to buy cigarettes in North Harrow.

On the way, a boy of about sixteen called me over from
the other side of the street. I had seen him and his crowd on
several occasions, though I didn't know his name or where
he came from. He was surrounded by a gang of kids, all a
little younger than me, ranging in age from ten to thirteen.
They had the appearance of a pack of hyenas who spent
their time circling our group whenever we played cards on
the grass in the evening.

As soon as I crossed over to him, he took hold of my
handlebars to stop me from escaping. His gang grabbed me,
making it impossible for me to move. This big lug then
punched me in the mouth. I felt his large, chunky ring
painfully jab into my gums.

'Give this message to your mates. This is what they're
gonna get if they don't watch out,' said the pack leader. After
being pushed and shoved from one to another, they let me
go with a chorus of jeers and mocking laughter.

I told the others what had happened and was surprised
that the boys reacted with such anger. Apparently, the bully
was another pupil from John Lyon School.

Several weeks later, he was found in the park with both
his arms broken. His mother, suspecting who had carried
out the punishment, actually thanked the boys for teaching

her son a lesson. He had become rude and nasty to her, and the beating had knocked the wind out of his sails. He had obviously been a serious thorn in several people's sides.

There was another Martin who was entirely different and who I really liked. One could say he was 'real'. His six-feet height may have been intimidating to some, but he was as gentle as he was true. Then there was Eccles, whose actual name I never knew before everything fell apart. Everyone in the group made me feel like I was part of something, and I had a great time getting drunk, listening to jazz, going to parties, and being sick.

It was at Martin Bright's all-night party that I got drunk for the very first time. I had been a little squiffy before on homemade potato wine, but this time, it was different.

It was a first for several reasons: It was the first all-night party that I had been to. It was the first time that I drank Beaujolais and Cherry Heering, the first time I was sick from drinking too much, and the first and last time that I got alcohol poisoning, or something very much like it.

One of the great things about that night was that Martin had an LP of King Oliver's Dixie Syncopators, Volume Two. I had Volume One. A small thing in itself, but for me, it was a kind of bonding as we discovered that we both loved early Black jazz. Although I was only thirteen, in the three years since I'd bought my first jazz record, I had become a diehard fan and connoisseur of the music.

I had at last found a place where I could be myself and not be laughed at for being cranky, and it was a refuge from the malaise that seemed to run through my family life. What has always surprised me was that I was accepted without any apparent disdain despite being a couple of years younger and from an entirely different background to many of them.

I believe that Martin was the only one who had a regular girlfriend, but whenever the group met to go somewhere, there were always two girls, Zoe and Hilary. Tagging along. Both wore their hair in the fashion of the time, a bizarre high bouffant. Hilary often capped hers with a head scarf. They hardly ever spoke to any of the company when we went out, and on never did they acknowledge me.

They were a constant presence for about eighteen months. Hilary was treated cruelly one evening, and I didn't see her again. Zoe remained on the scene for several more years but still refused to acknowledge my existence.

Most of the time, I met the crowd in a coffee bar in North Harrow, which was a new thing in those days—frothy coffee with cinnamon sprinkled on top, an old-fashioned cappuccino, but as the crowd got older, the pub over the road became a more enticing venue.

One evening, plucking up the courage to enter the pub with the others when I was just fifteen, I boldly asked for a half pint of bitter, and amazingly, I was served. On Christmas Eve, while standing in the Headstone Public House in North Harrow with a pint of bitter in front of me, the police suddenly charged in and rounded up all the underage drinkers.

Eccles shoved my glass into my hand and said, 'Don't take it away from your face.'

As I watched over the top of my pint, about a dozen youngsters, some older than I, were unceremoniously thrown out of the pub. One of the policemen decided to be a little more thorough and glanced in the direction of our group, but seeing nothing unusual, he turned and followed his fellows outside. That was a bit close, I thought, but it was to form a pattern until I was eighteen and could drink legally.

On another evening, we arrived at the pub dressed up in our usual not-so-usual clothes. We were ushered into a wedding reception, given seats at one of the long tables, and offered whatever we wanted in the way of food and drink at the buffet. We ate, drank, and had a really good time but never found out who it was that got married.

I had already discovered that to remain anonymous, all one had to do was dress up or down, depending on how an outsider perceived it. So on that particular evening, I was wearing the clothes that I had bought at a jumble sale the previous week—a coat with tails and a smart, white, dimpled-cotton waistcoat with lapels. This was set off with a pair of old school trousers that I had sewn into drainpipes with red cotton cross-stitching on the outer seams.

I might have appeared bizarre, but people only ever saw the cloak and never looked for the child within. I was never asked to state my age at any pub in any town from the age of fifteen onward.

In the summer of 1958, rumour had it that Frankie Barr's gang from Wembley and our local crew were set for a showdown in our park. The date had been fixed for a Saturday at

11am, and out of curiosity more than bravado, I went along to observe. I thought that it was going to be a small ruck, but I was totally overwhelmed by the sheer numbers that turned up.

There were about 150 young men, aged between 17 and 25, most of whom were armed. The weaponry ranged from small knives, cutthroat razors, and clubs to knuckle dusters, belts with nails pierced through them, and bicycle chains. One person had made up about fifteen fertiliser grenades while another had a pistol. I think it was a .38 service revolver, which were quite common after the war. Even my father had one.

I had never met most of the people that were there, but I soon understood that they were all part of the affiliation of gangs within our area. They freely conversed with each other, showing off their hardware.

I stood on the periphery, warily keeping an eye open in case it was necessary for me to quickly disappear.

A young chap stood next to me and declared that he didn't recognise anyone there. I asked him where he came from.

'Wembley,' he replied.

'Are you with Frankie's lot?' I asked.

He nodded, and as casually as I could, I told him that he was probably the only one of them there. He quietly slipped out of the park.

The fight never took place, and after about an hour and a half, the group gradually dispersed. The lad with the grenades blew several foot-deep holes in the cricket pitch as a parting gesture. Each bomb was filled with nails, sugar, and fertiliser rammed into the length of a bicycle handlebar tubing and was ignited with a short Jetex fuse.

Just before he left the park, he placed one on top of a post, and as the fuse burned away, two small children wandered up to it and watched it burn. Before anybody had a chance to pull them away, it blew up.

Fortunately, because they were so small and directly beneath the post, the blast missed them, although they were not just a little frightened by the explosion. We checked that they were okay, and off they went to the playground.

I had met Frankie at a party in Stanmore the previous year. One of the John Lyon fraternities was celebrating his birthday, and most of our group turned up for the occasion. Frankie arrived in a Simca Aronde followed by his friends in other vehicles. The car, though not large, slowly emptied its cargo. Out they came, one by one—the most amazing array of beautiful young women.

I still find it difficult to believe that there were so many of them in one car. They were the most elegant girls I had ever seen, all dressed in delightful cotton or silk summer prints. Daintily, they straightened themselves out and slinked into the party.

The party was in full swing, and most of the guests were having a great time. One of the young women took me under her wing for a couple of hours. I got the sense that she thought I needed looking after, a perk of being much younger than the others, until she was taken away by one of Frankie's gang. Then everything began to go terribly wrong.

A fight broke out in the sitting room, and one of the brawlers, in a Tarzan-like feat of idiocy to swing across the room, jumped for the large, crystal chandelier hanging from the ceiling, which shockingly crashed to the floor in pieces.

Another aggressor tried to punch somebody in the face through a pane of glass and severed an artery in his wrist. Blood squirted over the ceiling, up and down the walls, over the floor, and over anybody who was near him. Two of the girls managed to stop the flow, and he was carted off to hospital in an ambulance.

Frankie's second in command, a wiry, malevolent man dressed in a vest and gaudy braces that hitched up his trousers, demanded, in no uncertain terms, that everyone empty their pockets in a whip-round to pay for the damage done to the house. He was not somebody to argue with, having a particularly nasty persona, and nearly everyone paid up. As soon as his collection was finished, he disappeared, along with the money.

I left around eleven o'clock, somewhat relieved to be out of the place, and walked home.

A lot of crazy incidents occurred during that time. There was a lot of fighting, and some very bad elements infiltrated the old just-here-for-the-good-times attitude that once prevailed.

Nineteen-sixty saw the eventual breakup of my group of friends after an argument of some kind, and I had to find other things to do, some of which put me into a few tight spots which, in retrospect, were just a part of growing up—at least in my world.

17

The standard of teaching at Kilburn Polytechnic was brilliant, and being able to start both French and maths from the very beginning had a distinct advantage, not that I would ever excel at either. It was a commercially biased school with a view to pushing students through the initial two-year course and out into the world of banking or business. The further education department took in those who wanted to stay on to do O and A levels, giving some the chance of going to a university.

Instead of the usual history course, we did social and economic history, which was taught by an interesting and dedicated teacher in his late thirties. Mr Stern had a noticeable leaning to the left, politically speaking, and could also be described as being a little existential. However, sartorially speaking, he didn't have a great deal of sense, and on occasion would appear with a tie for a belt and his trouser zip undone. Such things were not important; it was the lesson that mattered.

At the end of the second year, he invited some of us to tea at his flat. He offered us such delicacies as a specialist tea, sandwiches, and Chinese gooseberries which were decidedly beige in colour with the fruit inside rather overripe. These are now called kiwi fruit, the name probably changed for commercial reasons, namely the fear of communism in the west. It may have been thought that they were made from propaganda manure and could contaminate anybody who might partake of them. To me, they will always be Chinese gooseberries.

To finish the tea, he produced a bottle of poitin which, like the fruit, had also changed colour. Originally, it had been clear as water when he bought it from a man in a Kilburn pub some months earlier, but it had now changed to a pale purple. He couldn't explain why. It didn't taste or smell like methylated spirit, and being always ready for a drink, I can safely say it didn't taste like one either, but by Jove, was it strong!

The business arithmetic teacher was equally extraordinary. He taught us how to multiply in our heads two columns of five numbers with a time limit of about twenty seconds. I can't do it now, but he managed to get the whole class to do it then, along with other mind-jabbing exercises.

One of his proudest moments was when he told us about his shoes. He had bought them in 1937 and had lovingly cared for them. He had them repaired when necessary, and even had parts re-stitched. He had waxed and polished them every day. But the leather, despite its amazing patina, began to crack. After all, it was 1957, and they were already twenty years old. It's sad to think that when the lower school closed down a couple of years later, it probably coincided with the death of his shoes.

One of our English teachers had previously been teaching children in Mexico. She was a woman of very high spirits, exuberant and, above all, someone who was able to enthuse the kids in class.

One day during a second-year lesson, the pestilential boy who sat in front of me turned around and proceeded to bend one of my fingers back as far as it would go, grinning like a baboon as he did so. It seemed like he was solely put on the earth to aggravate people without any apparent cause.

My measured response was to punch him fairly and squarely on his nose, and having done so, I suddenly became aware that the lesson had paused for a moment. Miss Dowdle was silent but had observed the whole incident with a glint of humour over the top of her glasses. The lesson continued from where she had left off without a word of reproach. I was quite impressed by her fairness.

She didn't last too long at Kilburn after falling foul of the headmaster, Mr Hemstock. It was coming up to Christmas, and she had worked hard getting us ready to perform one of Shakespeare's comedies for the end of term entertainment.

The headmaster appeared during one of the last rehearsals and declared that there was a change of plan, and the play could not go on. Her immediate response was one of utter disbelief and disgust that he could so glibly write off all the work that she and the class had done for the show.

Being of high spirits and not one to be cowed by inferior beings, she aimed a series of strong and extremely rude expressions at him, all of which I think were fair. She packed her bag then and there, apologised to us kids for wasting our time, and left. And that was the end of that. She was gone.

Following her was probably the most sexually alluring teacher in the whole of Britain or even possibly, in the world. To a fourteen-year-old boy confronted by a siren in high heels, with the occasional glimpse of her stocking tops—well, I can only say that over that period, my absorption of the English language slowed right down. She was only there for a couple of terms, which was quite disappointing.

It was unfortunate that so many teachers came and went. Those who were permanent were particularly good, and some of the temporary ones were as well, but there was one that didn't hit the mark. He was a Polish cavalry officer who, I presumed, had reached Britain during the war. He was an arrogant man, having a real problem with his overbearing sense of superiority.

During my second year at the school, I had been made a prefect and was trying to keep the dinner queue in some kind of order. I was on the tall flight of stone stairs that led down to the canteen when this taskmaster came down. Before I had a chance to move aside, he pushed me with some force, which sent me sprawling down the stairs and ending up on my back at the bottom.

Picking myself up, I demanded to know why he had pushed me, to which he replied, 'You were in my way!' Off he went without an apology. During the following school holiday, he was arrested for raping a young girl on Harrow Hill. So he, too, never returned to Kilburn Poly.

Probably the most dynamic personality in the school was one of the maths teachers, Mr Costello. He knew his subject very well but delivered it in such a way that the underlying element of fear would always dog one's ability to learn.

His style was twofold: firstly, he was volatile, and secondly, he was dogmatically controlling. He was also the boys' games instructor with an unsuppressed appetite for watching the boys in the communal bath at the Welsh Harp playing fields near Neasden.

I never liked football or cricket, the first because I couldn't see any sense in standing around in the snow in a pair of cotton shorts and a tee-shirt while a couple of heroes pranced around in the middle of the field. For the latter, idling in the blazing sun in a pair of long white trousers, a shirt, and a white jersey watching a couple of clever dicks knocking the ball about, over and over, was torturous when all you really wanted to do was go to sleep under a tree. Give me a good run any day; anybody can join in, and nobody really has to win.

Now in the scheme of things, if one doesn't like something, one shouldn't have to pay into it, least of all under duress. Bearing that in mind, I saw absolutely no reason why I should buy a Schoolboys' International Football ticket, especially since I was never going to use it. Another consideration was that I didn't have the three shillings and sixpence for the damned thing, and I thought it was very expensive.

Mr Costello put it to us that it was our duty to buy at least one ticket each 'in support of the school', but in reality, he was on an ego trip to say that he had a full house. Most of the boys paid up within a few days; others tarried for a couple of weeks. Three or four paid up after about three weeks, leaving one person who had not.

The double maths lesson commenced with two teachers at the head of the classroom: Mr Anderson, our regular teacher, and Mr Costello. The agenda was not mathematics but, 'What a disgrace that there is one person who has not bought a ticket.'

It was a hard lesson for everybody, but particularly for me, as I had to stand on a chair with my hands on my head for a whole ninety minutes. I was cajoled and asked to explain why, and how could I let everybody down, not that my excuses were of any interest to them. This was followed by the second phase: anger, shouting, and professed disgust, both of them berating me at once. It was all getting rather boring, and having gone this far, I was not going to be beaten down with their threats.

At the end of the session, having got absolutely nowhere with me, Costello finally changed tactics completely and begged me---as a personal favour to him and seemingly apologetic for having subjected me to such a tirade---to buy a ticket.

I acquiesced, rightly or wrongly, but I had a feeling that somehow, I had scored a serious victory. Costello had met his match for once and strangely appreciated my determination. The outcome was much to my personal advantage and from which I was to benefit later in the further education segment at the polytechnic.

On the playing field, he was in his element. The chance to embrocate the boys was never missed. However, he was good at discipline, not physically punitive but strong enough to break up any dispute that took place on the field. I saw him on one occasion pick two fifteen-year-olds up off the ground, one in each hand, and carry them off the field like a pair of crabs, his arms outstretched and showing no sign of strain. He was holding easily a hundred weight in each hand. I was impressed.

My contribution to football was very small. I was always at the back by the goal. As I said before, the game rarely came away from the centre of the pitch. In frustration and feeling seriously cold, every now and again, I would sally forth like Don Quixote. Running down the field, scattering all before me, I'd race across the pitch, my skinny legs capped with old-fashioned football boots and my long arms flailing like a windmill. To the others, I had the appearance of an unruly weapon, a kind of Exocet missile, and nobody dared to get in my way. Tackling me was not on offer.

With a mighty kick, I would either miss the ball completely and fall over or kick it straight offside. I would then wander back to my previous position and lean against the goal post feeling just a little bit warmer.

At home, it was becoming increasingly difficult to do my homework. In the evening, the television was perpetually on in the living room, and in my bedroom, there was not enough room in the lower bunk bed to sit in an upright position. Sitting on the upper one, I found it too uncomfortable to have my legs out in front of me or dangling over the edge for any length of time. I therefore used the only other room available, barring the lavatory, in which to do my work.

My parents' bedroom was the largest room in the flat and had an electric convector heater and a large radiogram. It was also quite peaceful, being at the opposite side of the flat. My father had rigged up some kind of wiring which joined the television to the radiogram speakers, the idea being that records could be played and heard in both the living room and the bedroom. I usually played some jazz as I worked, and not realising that the switch that isolated the television from the radiogram was still in the on position, I proceeded to put a disc on the turntable.

I remember only too well that I had one hand on the electric fire as I touched the gram's centre spindle.

The shock was massive. I was thrown the total length of the room and crashed into the headboard of the bed at the other side. Stunned, I lay there wondering what on earth had happened.

Earth was the operative word. I had earthed the television, the radiogram, and the electric fire all at once and consequently took a flying lesson. Not much fun in an enclosed space, I might add. Pale as death and shivering with the shock, I went into the living room to tell my parents what had happened.

Without veering their eyes from the telly, my father simply said, 'You shouldn't have been touching the electric fire.'

The gram was never disconnected from the television despite not being used for the purpose my father had intended, but I always made sure that the electric fire was sufficiently far away if ever I played any records there again.

18

During the first year of lower school at Kilburn Poly, we got the opportunity to go to Switzerland for Easter break. I was surprised that my parents were so keen on the trip that they came up with the thirty pounds needed for it. Clearly, it was a convenient way to get me off their hands for a few days while also avoiding the appearance of poverty.

On leaving the train at Dover from London, an incredibly boring episode, the group eagerly clambered aboard the ferry bound for Calais.

Ferries in those days were not the same as today's and might be described as basic. Travelling third class, there were only wooden benches to sit on inside a metal area without windows, and we soon set about exploring other parts of the boat.

Once we were well underway, the weather suddenly broke, and a storm swept across the Channel, causing our little tub to rock unmercifully amid the turbulent waves. Even some of the stewards were sick, and puke swept backwards and forwards along the metal floors.

Bowls were thrown onto tables as receptacles for those unable to get to the loo, and pale green faces loomed here and there before slipping away as another wave sent the ship pitching over. Hardly anybody was spared from being sick, and I think the cleaners at Calais really had a job on their hands when we docked.

The group, which included some girls from the Colindale annexe to Kilburn Poly, was led by our French teacher, Mr Lipton, who not only spoke French fluently but was singularly noticeable by the habitual accessory of a grey plastic Pac-a-Mac. Even at night, while checking that we had all settled down in our rooms, he would appear at the door or in the corridor in this apparel.

It was an adventure as I had never been outside the UK before. Taking the train to Strasbourg, we commenced our trip and forgot all about the gruelling ferry crossing. We passed through the industrial zones in northern France where the fires from the furnaces gave the impression that whole towns were alight.

After Strasbourg, we arrived at Basle, where we spilled out of the train and into the slick but busy Swiss lavatories. Suddenly, the door to the gents' WC opened, and in walked a woman! Many a knee buckled and many a stream stopped in its emiction. This was, after all, 1957, and it just wasn't a British habit, and neither was she.

Unabashed, she walked over to a wash basin and wet a cloth before bidding us *bonjour*, leaving those who hadn't had time to do up their trousers frozen in place. This was the precursor to the strange world of the Swiss as seen from innocent English eyes.

Off we went on another train to Montreux on the edge of Lake Geneva to find our hotel and unload our baggage in our allotted rooms. My room, which I shared with two other boys, overlooked a railway cutting, above which ran the overhead electric cables that powered the trains, sparking and clattering every time a train whooshed by.

We assembled for our first Swiss meal, seated at long tables in a dimly lit canteen. The staff hurried about serving up freshly made leak and potato soup, which was quickly devoured with chunks of French bread, and then came the main course.

There was a look of consternation on the faces of the staff as, one by one, the kids pushed their plates away. The overwhelming bouquet of garlic pervaded the cafeteria, and it was only the brave who ventured to eat the food.

Despite being ultra-thin, I was perpetually hungry with an astonishing appetite that could at times make a dog blanche. At that time, I would eat nearly everything that came my way, including the food that the others had rejected.

Thus ended the first day, with my hunger fully sated and the rest bemoaning the lack of English cuisine. During the days ahead, the cook presented us with snail vol-au-vents and slightly undercooked liver among other delicacies, all beautifully garnished with plenty of garlic. Mr Lipton had a chat with the housekeeper, and disappointed, the cook agreed to feed us in the future with a less toxic menu.

A few trips up into the foothills and mountains had been organised, which were memorable, not for the brooding darkness that pervaded the alps, but more for the curious behaviour of the Swiss.

Coming from Britain where most houses had running water, even if the loos were at the bottom of the garden, it was a bit of a shock in the town of Gruyère to see women washing their laundry in the village fountain, pummelling the garments against the stones. But it was amusing to see the scattered boxes of OMO or DAZ, a kind of acknowledgement that the twentieth century was seeping in.

On another trip to a tourist centre that overlooked the Mont Blanc massif, a familiar event took place. In the past, it had been a regular occurrence for me to be attacked by dogs. Normally they were quite small dogs—poodles, Scotties, terriers, sometimes an Alsatian or Labrador—but never before had I been leaped upon by a St. Bernard. The dog was about twice my size, its teeth bared and jaws dripping slime. With this occurring on top of a mountain, my chances of escape were somewhat diminished, unless, of course, I jumped into a chasm, which was equally unappealing.

The dog's owner soon arrived, and heaving the snarling beast away, he gave me the typical what-did-you-do-to-my-dog look.

In the days that followed, such an event dissipated into insignificance. We had plenty of spare time, and off we'd go in groups to explore the town of Montreux.

We were warned not to go to a particular gift shop where a seemingly kind and helpful man was often observed looking in the window or loitering inside the shop. He would offer to translate for the shopkeeper, inform customers of the purchase price, then return some of the change to the shopper and pocket the rest. He managed to divest nearly all of us of a few Swiss francs. He must have been working in liaison with the shopkeeper to continue to run this scam the whole time we were there.

One sunny afternoon, about ten of us decided to go horse riding at a stable just outside the town. Because most of the group had never been on a horse before, we chose the safe option of riding around in a circle inside a large barn. The horses were massive and not well behaved.

I had no idea how to steer or stop my horse, which often led it to trot too close to the one in front. The horse in front would then attempt to kick mine in the face, which would cause my horse to suddenly rear up and throw me off.

The first time was amazing; it was a real circus stunt. The horse reared, I flew up into the air, somersaulted, and landed standing up, as if I did it for a living. The second time, I did a sideways flip and landed in a crouching position, arms outstretched as you would see in a proper performance. The third time, I got my comeuppance by landing, without any fancy acrobatics, flat on my back.

Each time I came off, the proprietor insisted that I should remount, but after the third fall, I refused. I thought it was getting too dangerous, and I didn't like flying too much either. This did not please the boss at all, and handing his long ringmaster's whip to his stable boy, he told the lad to show me what he was made of.

The earth flying up in front of me as the boy cracked the whip did not actually impress me very much. Little by little, he got closer and closer, flicking the ground right up to my feet. I thought to myself that if he really pushed it, he being smaller than I, he could have a serious problem on his hands. I didn't care for this kind of intimidation one bit, especially as I was being charged for it.

In the meantime, the horses continued to trot around the barn and only stopped when one of the girls was thrown from her mount and hurt her back. The horses were then led away, and the lesson seemed to have concluded—but no! The ringmaster had one more trick to show us.

The stable boy, having given the whip back to his boss, returned with a small pony, not unlike a Shetland pony, and his employer encouraged the group to pet the animal. I chose not to, being in no mood to continue with this farce. The man then helped one of the kids to sit on the little creature, which was already a little agitated.

Walking away, he stooped, picked up a clod of earth, and threw it at the rump of the pony. The horse shot off, depositing its rider in the mud. Insisting that everybody should join in the fun, he forced each one of us to mount and be thrown off in the same manner, except for me and the injured girl.

She was a delight to look at, and I had already developed a crush on her from the start, but I was clueless as to how to approach her. She was a year older than I, which felt a bit intimidating.

Eventually, the hour was up, and our muddy entourage queued up to pay. The proprietor grudgingly took my money, muttering something that sounded like an insult, as if it wasn't enough for his troubles.

One afternoon, our group decided to go boating. There were rowing boats and pedalos, and while the others stayed in the vicinity of the boating station, two of us took a pedalo and set off across the lake.

It didn't look that far, and after an hour or so, we were still only halfway across. Montreux had become no more than a distant image. The wind had changed, and the water had become decidedly choppy, so we gave up the idea and turned the pedalo around to return to the boat station. The faster we peddled, the slower we seemed to go, and with the wind blowing against us, it took another couple of hours to get back.

Mr Lipton was frantic with worry, and in his great relief, he slapped me and gave me his neatly rolled up Pac-a-Mac to carry. We all returned to the pension for our supper.

Apparently, during the afternoon, we had missed the real fun. One of the boys, the stinky one from the English class, had the misfortune to upset several of the others. In return, some of the lads set out in a couple of rowing boats and rammed his boat again and again until it sank. The boy had to be rescued from the sinking vessel by the boat owner. The others would have let him go down with the wreck, but it probably wouldn't have been a good idea. It would have upset his parents, I'm sure.

The boatman was furious. He had lost one boat and was sure that our pedalo had gone as well. On our return, he permanently banned all of us from his enclosure.

I was often accused of having an overactive imagination, which frustrated me since they only needed to open their eyes and look to confirm what I saw. So many interesting things are missed because people lack curiosity or simply don't bother to look.

I love to just sit and observe my surroundings. One evening after dinner, I was looking out the window towards the railway lines and the bridge on the right. On one side of the bridge were some bushes which flanked the road.

My attention was drawn to the clacking of a woman's high heels as she approached. I watched her as she crossed over to the other side of the bridge where she stopped. I saw a man emerge from the bushes and walk over to her. I thought this was rather interesting and said to my room-mates, 'Come and have a look at this!'

I told them what I had seen, to which they both replied, 'Arh, you won't catch us like that!'

I satisfied myself by giving them a running commentary as the scene unfolded. The man and the woman began to quarrel, and a fairly violent struggle ensued. After a short period, the man disappeared once more into the bushes. The woman lingered a while until another man arrived. As they talked, the one in the bushes re-emerged, and the three stood together in conversation.

The light by this time had more or less gone, and the streetlight on the bridge was not bright enough for me to see the conclusion of this slightly bizarre episode. My two roommates were chortling away, ridiculing every turn in my narration of the events, calling me a liar and other disparaging remarks, until I could take no more and lost my temper.

I leaped on top of them as they lay under the bed covers together, sniggering. Having exerted a certain degree of violence, I finally calmed down and went to my own bed. Hearing the commotion, Mr Lipton appeared in the doorway in his grey plastic Pac-a-Mac, but all was quiet. He closed the window and inquired if we had cleaned our teeth, then left the room, regarding us with some suspicion as he went.

I decided that I did not much like mountains. The perpetual darkness of their looming over the lake and their cold, brooding silence were not to my taste.

We visited Château de Chillon on the edge of Lake Geneva, which was much more interesting, and as I crossed the footbridge to the castle, I felt something slip down my right leg. As I looked down, I saw my last Swiss franc disappear into the water below and found, to my dismay, a small hole in my pocket and my last remaining francs gone. It was a bit of a disappointment which was only alleviated by being in the company of the girl on the horse.

When the morning of our departure arrived, the hotel provided us with a packed lunch, a banana, and a couple of sandwiches, which I finished off before we left the Swiss border. I braced myself to starve until we reached London, which was going to take several hours, with no money to buy a snack on the way.

However, the great consolation was that during the long journey, the object of my desire lay her head on my lap and dozed for several hours as we passed through France. I dared not move lest I break the spell and stayed awake all the way. Unfortunately, that spell was broken on reaching Calais, where we all dispersed, and I never saw her again. I didn't even know her name.

On reaching London, I was met by my brother, which was quite a surprise, and being totally parched, I longed for a cup of tea, even if it was a British Rail one. We entered the station cafeteria only to be told, 'Tea is off. We have run out.' I had never heard of an English café or cafeteria, particularly a railway one, run out of tea before.

I never gave up on the hope of finding that beautiful girl on the train at the Colindale annexe to Kilburn Poly. And so, the Swiss adventure faded into memory as other events infiltrated my smoke-filled days.

19

As familiarity turned to monotomy in North Harrow, and finding it impossible to buy the kind of jazz I liked in any of the record shops, I started to venture into London's West End. It was mid-1960, and I was now fifteen years old.

I discovered Doug Dobell's Jazz Record Shop on Charing Cross Road and decided it would be great to sit in a coffee bar and watch the world go by. I chose The House of Sam Widges on D'Arblay Street, a name I thought was quite amusing. I ordered a cappuccino and sat down.

The record I bought was 'In Harlem's Araby' by King Oliver's Memphis Jazzers. which to this day, fifty years on, is still one of my favourite pieces of jazz. I placed the 78 on the table in front of me and mused about all the jazz that I hadn't yet heard while, at the same time, discreetly viewing the comings and goings in the coffee bar.

My attention was drawn to a fairly well-built Black man wearing a smart dark hat, who was quietly talking to a smaller and rather agitated white man.

After a short while, the white guy passed a newspaper under the table and into the grasp of the other man who, removing some paper money from it, slipped something back inside and returned it in the same manner.

They continued to chat briefly while the item was cautiously removed from within the pages. Leaving the newspaper on the table. the white man rose, shook hands with the Black man, and left.

I don't know what possessed me to approach George, for that was his name, but I went over to him while he read the news and asked him if he knew my brother. Crazy as it might seem, I believed then that the whole of London, if not the whole bloody world, knew my brother.

George replied, 'No, I don't know him, but my friend Carl probably does.'

Using my school train pass for these excursions made going to the West End a cheap affair. Nobody ever checked my card at the barriers of any of the London stations at any time of day or night.

It was on my second or third foray into London that I met Carl for the first time. It was at the same coffee bar, Sam Widges, where I found Carl conversing with George. He was West African, like George, and had once been a boxer. He was still quite athletic and in his early thirties or so. I think George had forgotten who I was, so I introduced myself and found Carl to be quite an affable character.

After a short chat, George left, and Carl suggested that we make our way to the Champion Public House on Wells Street on the other side of Oxford Street. As we walked, we came to a building which was undergoing some repair.

When we passed under an exposed girder which jutted out above our heads, Carl jumped up and grabbed a small plastic bag from its hiding place. It looked as if it was full of sugar lumps, the ones that come two in a packet and can be found in a tea or coffee room.

He pushed it into my hand and said, 'Put it in your jacket pocket. It'll be safer there, and you're not so likely to get stopped. I'll see you in the Champion in a minute. You go straight on. I'm going to take another route,' and away he trotted.

I had not been to the Champion before. Opening the door, I was confronted by a mass of people, including a man dressed as an African king in full traditional robes and head-gear. This was the first time I had been in a London pub, and being only fifteen, I was a bit nervous.

I could see Carl across the saloon bar, and taking the bag out of my pocket, I held it up above my head and called out, 'Carl, Carl, here's your bag!'

In a moment of undiluted panic, Carl bolted towards me, and stuffing the packet inside his shirt, he anxiously glanced around to see if anybody had noticed. He calmed down, but it was at that point that I began to suspect it was not sugar lumps I had carried.

My relationship with Carl ended quite abruptly some weeks later, having only met him on three occasions. It was not his doing but his friendship with my brother that pre-cipitated the most frightening experience of my life.

I was nearly sixteen and on my way back from the Duke of York pub on Rathbone Street to catch the tube home after the pub's closing. My brother pulled up alongside me on his motor scooter and asked if I wanted a lift home. At first, I declined the offer, past experience having shown me how unreliable he was. I had my train pass and thought it would be better to go by tube. But I let him persuade me, and off we went.

Within a few minutes he called out, 'I have to call in at the As You Like It,' a late-night café near Shaftesbury Avenue. Carl was there, and we sat down with him to have a cup of coffee.

My brother suddenly declared, 'I'll be back in half an hour. I have to see somebody.'

Carl and I sat and waited. I assumed that my brother had picked up a message at the bar, and it was an hour and a half before my brother returned. The last train to Harrow had long gone.

Without so much as an apology or excuse, he said, 'I have to meet somebody. Back in a moment', and off he went again.

At 3.30am, Carl and I were asked to leave as the bar was about to close. Carl suggested that we go back to his place in Camden Town for the rest of the night, and so we started to walk.

At the bottom of Tottenham Court Road, there was an all-night kiosk selling cigarettes and sweets, and as we approached, Carl spotted a car parked at the curb that he thought he recognised.

He bent down to glance at the occupants, four Cypriots and an English boy, and was met with an aggressive 'oowa yer screwin'?' in other words, 'Who are you looking at?'

Carl, with an amazingly polite response, told them that he thought he had recognised their car, wanted to say hello, and apologised for his boldness.

His reply took the edge off their sharpness, and one of them inquired where we were going. Carl said that we were going to Camden Town.

One occupant said, 'We're going that way. Jump in. We'll give you a lift.'

I sat in the front, squashed against the door, with a brawny Cypriot beside me, his arm resting across my shoulders. Carl had squeezed into the back. It was far too tight for comfort.

As the car travelled along Tottenham Court Road, various pleasantries were exchanged. The English boy, only a little older than me, said that he was a student at the Northern Polytechnic, and I replied that I went to Kilburn Poly.

All seemed quite amicable until Carl noticed that the car was no longer going in the right direction. By this time, my too-close neighbour had started to grope me. At that moment, I heard one of the back-seat men address Carl.

'How would you like to be dead?'

Carl replied nonchalantly, 'Not very much.'

The same question was then addressed to me, and feeling distinctly uncomfortable and ready to scream, I replied, 'At this moment, I couldn't think of anything better'.

It was probably not the best response, as from the back came a grisly description of how they planned to dispose of me after doing what they intended. They were not interested in Carl. They were just going to murder him and dump his body. The bloodthirsty savage made it clear that my body was to be chucked in the Thames with a knife in my back after they had finished playing with me. I was appreciative that a more comprehensive description of their intentions was not forthcoming. I was scared enough as it was.

The car stopped at some traffic lights, and Carl shouted, 'Jump!' and I did. I shot up the road like a frightened rabbit. I dashed across the street and dived into the bushes of a large house's front garden. Beyond the garden lay a right-hand turning into another street. I hoped it would look from a distance as if I had run into the turning and vanished.

In the meantime, having seen me sprint up the road in the wrong direction, Carl had run around the car to give me more time, until they got hold of him and knocked him down into the gutter before driving off in pursuit of me, their real quarry.

From my hiding place, I saw the car crawl by, dark faces peering out in the glow of the streetlights, unsure of where I had disappeared. They continued to edge along the curb, and reaching the corner, turned right into the next street, just as I had hoped.

My heart was thundering, my chest heaving, gasping for air. I took a few seconds to collect myself, unsure of where I was, but with Death and Mayhem searching me out, I left my hiding place. Whimpering and shivering, I trotted back down the road in search of Carl.

As I approached the traffic lights, the point from where I had made my escape, an old van came round the corner. I ran out in front of it, and waving my arms, I yelled, 'Help!'

To my utmost joy and surprise, the van stopped, and a woman's voice screamed, 'Get out! Get out! I've had enough. I can't take anymore!'

The van door opened and out jumped Carl. The distressed woman slammed the van door and drove off. In fairness to her, being forced to stop her van on a deserted street at four o'clock in the morning and instructed to drive by a man she didn't know was an experience I'm sure she could have lived without.

Apparently, Carl had run out in front of her, and before she knew what was going on, he had opened the door and slid in beside her.

At least I was reunited with Carl. Not knowing where we were, we tried to retrace our journey to the Tottenham Court Road. As we walked, we met a man who, on hearing our story, agreed to walk with us and directed us back to the bright lights. He was an off-duty policeman, so he said, and was looking for a prostitute. In retrospect, he must have been searching for a particular woman for some reason, rather than just a casual sexual tryst.

As we walked with the officer, the car reappeared and slowly dogged our steps for about ten minutes before finally giving up and driving off. The appearance of the car had fortunately corroborated our story, and the man directed us to a uniformed beat officer who was to be at the top of the Tottenham Court Road at 5.25am.

Sure enough, the officer was at the designated place and took down the story. We had, of course, written down the car make and number when it reappeared, but the officer had a problem with the detail.

'How could you all get into such a vehicle?'

As he pondered, a black meat wagon came by. Two officers jumped out, opened the rear doors of the van, grabbed Carl, and threw him into the back of the van. They slammed the doors and said to the constable, 'Alright now, Jim?'

It may not have been Jim or Jack or even Rupert, but they called him by name, and he replied, 'Oh, it's all right. They were just reporting an incident.'

The other two unlocked the back of the van, grabbed hold of Carl once again, dragged him out to a standing position, brushed him down briefly, and said, 'Okay, mate!' and drove away.

The night had gone on far too long, and now being close to Delancey Street in Camden Town, I was relieved to reach the outer door to Carl's flat. He had a tiny bedsit on the top floor without any vestige of comfort. We sat there gloomily, and after all that had happened, I was still on edge and unable to relax. I was, to be honest, a little wary of Carl despite his courage. I also needed to pee.

The lavatory was outside in the hallway, and on reaching it, I realised that the nightmare had still not ended. The loo floor was two or three inches below the landing floor level, and as I stepped down, my shoes filled with urine and God knows what else. The lavatory was overflowing and had been for some while, but being desperate, I felt I had no option but to add my contribution to this awful state of affairs.

Late on the Sunday morning, I arrived home feeling distinctly spaced out and, I suppose, traumatised. I said nothing to my mother but noted that my brother had not returned home and didn't do so for the entire week.

Returning to Kilburn Poly the next day, I remembered I had told the English boy in the car that I was a student there, and for the next three months, I was in a state of acute anxiety when it was time to leave school.

Once a Cypriot in Kilburn High Road smiled and said, 'Hello. You okay?' which scared the pants off me. I can't think who he thought I was or why he thought that he knew me, unless ...

I accepted one more lift from my brother, during which, diverting as he always did, we ended up at a party somewhere in North London. He drove straight there, obviously knowing the location. He had 'to see somebody', and on joining the festivities, I slipped in behind the piano and dozed off, an easy thing to do with a few pints of Guinness and bitter under my belt.

Within half an hour, a rumpus started, and on awakening, I was amused to see my brother being pushed down the stairs by an angry group of partygoers, in whose company he had finally lost his composure. We left, he with a red face and twitching nose and I groggily giggling under my breath.

20

What is it that makes certain men think you want to have sex with them, regardless of your orientation? This is a common complaint from women but is not very often heard from the lips of a male. Now I can assure you right from the start that I am not fond of men, never have been, and so for them to have got the picture straight, I should have worn a sandwich board declaring 'DO NOT TOUCH' from the age of nine.

By the time I was sixteen, I could no longer go into a public lavatory and learned to hold my urine for hours. But sometimes, a visit to the loo became crucial to avoid embarrassment. It was on such an occasion when my girlfriend, Suzanne, and I had gone into the News Theatre in Trafalgar Square to be entertained by Tom and Jerry, Felix the Cat, and other amusing characters.

News Theatres were primarily cinemas whose programs consisted of forty minutes of news and an hour of cartoons which, if the weather was bad, offered a cheap afternoon diversion. Shortly after being seated, I found it necessary to visit the gents. As some may have an interest in the distinctive peculiarities of various toilets around the country, I will describe my personal experience at this particular loo.

Pushing the door open, I entered a cloakroom about twelve feet long, with a wooden bench along the left-hand wall below a row of coat hooks. Sitting quite still in the middle of the bench was a large man in a beige raincoat, apparently oblivious of my entry. Beyond this foyer was the urinal, a white tiled wall with a trough at its base, the whole room being no more than eight feet deep from the entrance.

At the left-hand end of the urinal was a man, perhaps twenty to twenty-five years old, masturbating. I thought to myself, *Don't take any notice. Just turn away, pee, and go.*

But Chance once more turned her back on me, and as I did the same and started to pee, a hand draped itself over my left shoulder, and a face peered down at my penis.

Fear and rage erupted, and with volcanic violence, I threw the intruder against the wall and, for a few seconds, lost all sense of reality. When the mist cleared, I could see the man slowly slipping down the wall, his tongue hanging limply from his mouth, and his head lolling to one side.

I quickly felt for my pocketknife. It was still there. Somehow, I had managed to button up my trousers. My face and body ached as if I had undergone an immense struggle or metamorphosis, every tendon stretched to its limit. I turned and ran.

The man in the foyer was still there. Passing him, I crashed through the door and raced off towards the back exit of the cinema as if all the demons in hell were after me.

Seeing my flight, Suzanne quickly left her seat and caught up with me as I struggled in panic to open the fire doors. They finally gave way, and we scurried off into the afternoon crowds.

Recalling the events shortly afterwards, I realised that as I left the WC, I had passed a queue of men waiting by the door. Since the cinema was barely occupied, and there was no shortage of seats, were they all waiting to take turns with me?

What damage I did to the man, I will never know. He certainly did not look well, but I think it is extraordinary that in situations of extreme stress, the body can summon immense power far beyond one's ability. Stories abound of people who cannot explain how they managed to save somebody's life by acquiring some metaphysical power which they had conjured up from nowhere. If only it could be relied upon to show itself every time it was needed.

In another incident, I had arrived at Kilburn Poly one morning, and realising that my intestines were about to erupt, I decided to return home. The walk back to Kilburn station was bad enough, and waiting for the train was even worse, particularly when I became aware that I was attracting some unwanted attention.

The train arrived, and verifying that this gentleman was definitely on my case, I waited on the platform until the last instant before the doors closed. He was quick and managed to get into the carriage. I had to change trains at Wembley Park and quickly slipped into the lavatory on the platform to indulge in a game of hide and seek while waiting for my connection to North Harrow.

At that time, the Gents was a long room with urinals on both sides and a double bank of cubicles in the centre.

As the man followed me in along one side, I slipped round to the other and quickly and quietly left the toilet. I could hear his footsteps pacing slowly back and forth, probably thinking I had gone into one of the cubicles.

The metropolitan line train arrived, and diving into it as the doors were about to close, I felt safe at last.

This particular gentleman did not know how lucky he was to have had such a narrow escape. It was not that I would have hurt him, but had he grabbed me, he could have been blanketed by an explosive deluge of diarrhoea, me included. On such occasions, maybe I should have worn a sandwich board saying, 'DO NOT TOUCH, EXPLOSIVE!'

My father had bought a 1937 Austin 16 with green mudguards and a black body. It was a large, cumbersome vehicle and was, as far as I knew, the only one in the area. It had been stored since 1939, at the outbreak of war, and had registered less than 20,000 miles on the clock.

At 7.30 one morning during the school summer holiday, I was walking towards Wealdstone on my way to work at Advance Laundry, when it started to rain. A car identical to my father's pulled up beside me, and the driver called out, 'Want a lift? I see you every morning. Jump in. I'll drop you off at Wealdstone.'

The man was dressed in a blue overall, just like my father, and he looked as if he were a mechanic. He was also about my father's size and age.

I got into the car and was ready to discuss with the driver the qualities of his vehicle in comparison to my father's car when, within a few minutes, he casually posed the question, 'How big is it now?'

'How big is what?'

'Don't give me that. You know what I mean. How big is it?'

'What,' I reiterated. And then the penny dropped.

'You know...IT?' he said angrily.

My only response was to put my feet up on the leather seat, hug my knees and say, 'I don't know. I have never bothered to measure it. Now stop and let me out!'

He drove on for another mile without saying a word, finally stopping on the road to Kenton and cursing me for leading him on. And all that before eight o'clock in the morning!

I would like to say that my desirability faded as I got older, but it didn't. It continued with aggravating regularity, with young men eyeing me with salacious delight and old ones giving me 'the look'. That useful phrase—sod off—in most cases, would've sufficed, but occasionally, there were conspirators out there who would not be so easily dissuaded.

By age 36, I had become a self-employed restorer of antique furniture and had been asked by a client to have a look at his stored antiques to either buy or restore. The young man, a few years younger than I, had been to my workshop and appeared keen to learn how to do some of the work himself, and I was quite happy to give him some guidance.

His collection of furniture had been transferred to a building in Cornfield Terrace in St. Leonards-on-Sea near my workshop, and at an agreed time, I arrived to meet him.

As I entered the room, I was immediately aware of a couple of the local youths—Miles, a light-fingered 'queen', and his faithful companion, Kevin. The proprietor of the store made his appearance, sharply dressed in black and white two-tone brogues and immaculately cut suit, his face pink as if he had just shaved. I began to feel a little uneasy, and the shop owner, prevaricating, seemed to be playing for time as more youngsters arrived, most of whom I knew to be gay.

I noticed that several stood in front of the main door, as if barring the exit should I try to escape. Sensing that something untoward was about to happen, I walked toward those at the door and said, 'There may be a lot of you, but if you try to stop me from leaving, I will seriously hurt you.' They stepped aside, and I opened the door and left.

A couple of weeks later, I met the young shopkeeper's sister, who informed me that he had hanged himself a few days before.

These events took place over a period of some years and, therefore, gave me the time to put each one out of mind before the next occurred. Writing them down all together seems to make them sound more egregious than perhaps they were. To put them into context, one only has to think of how many young women and girls were regularly molested or raped around railway stations and on trains during the fifties, sixties and later. I survived, but a lot of young women didn't.

21

During the months following the Cypriot affair, everything became a jumble. I had stopped going to London for a while and spent more time around the Queen's Head public house in Pinner without anything dramatic happening that I choose to remember.

In my wanderings, I had met some people involved in the emerging popularity of American folk music and was invited to an afternoon gathering at a house in Harrow.

Within a week, I had been quickly introduced to others and ended up at a pub on Shaftesbury Avenue in Harrow the following Saturday night. I was plied with beer for a couple of hours without paying for a single drink. Just before closing time, I was handed a large tin of white emulsion paint and a one-inch paintbrush.

At this point, I realised that I had become part of something more than just an evening out, as seen through the bottom of a glass, and that plans had already been made which required the tin I now carried. Two of the group had been chosen to paint on North Harrow railway bridge whilst my group was to paint on the Shaftesbury Avenue railway bridge. One other group went off somewhere else.

I was in the group led by the mastermind of the operation, who owned a Heinkel bubble car. Three of us stuffed ourselves into this minuscule vehicle which careened all over the road, and we eventually arrived at our destination. Our ringleader was to be the lookout while the other guy and I were to be the painters.

The target for the evening was the increased use of English territory by the United States military and the creation of Panzer tank bases in Germany, which we saw as being an escalation of the Cold War.

Still unsteady from the evening's alcohol, I started to scrawl 'BAN U.S. AND PANZER BASES' on the brickwork. Before I could finish, a car pulled up, and two men ran at us with pickax handles. I thought to myself that the tin of paint would have to do as a safeguard should I be attacked.

The two men stopped, and one shouted, 'Police! Put the paint down!'

Thanks to the lookout who had just one job and failed, we were nabbed, paint in hand, by two off-duty policemen on their way home from work. What had not been taken into account in the planning of the mission was the proximity of the police headquarters, which was just a few hundred yards down the road.

We were taken to Harrow police station and placed in a cell for the night. The cells were tucked away at the back of the station and were the original Victorian model, not unlike a cage with vertical iron bars running the length of the room with one section sliding back for access.

The uniformed staff were quite amused at their little catch, not the usual Saturday night drunks but three radicals, one in fancy dress with long hair who puffed away at a Swiss pipe, one looking like a French Apache dancer, and the other an argumentative left-wing activist who constantly berated the officers for having arrested us with little thought to the effect on world safety. The police offered us tea, and because I was still not sixteen, they telephoned my parents to collect me, which was rather unfortunate.

At home, my mother slapped me and said, 'I hope you're proud of yourself!'—meaning, of course, that she hoped I was proud of myself for bringing such disgrace upon the family. My response was a resounding, 'YES!'

Funny how, when my brother stole a pint of milk from a crate outside a café in the middle of the night—despite having a pocket full of money and a milk machine nearby—the police seemed to shrug it off. My parents dismissed it as just a harmless prank. They didn't consider that, following a complaint from the café owner who kept losing milk at night, the police kept watch to catch the thief, and we all knew who that was. He was no longer a boy either—he was nineteen years old.

The end result was that I began to take a more serious view of the nuclear arms question and became more entrenched in my personal view of the world, not that this interested anyone at home.

Following my arrest, the three of us were dragged before the Tory magistrate at Harrow Magistrates' Court. We had been charged with malicious damage, a misleading term which I think should be redefined. We may have caused some minor damage to the brickwork, but 'malicious' suggested that we had purposefully gone out to destroy the bricks, which was total rubbish.

A representative of the London Transport Executive was called in from Southampton to look at the wall and to assess the damage. We were to pay the costs of his travel, his time, and for the repair of the wall. I questioned why somebody had to travel seventy odd miles each way to look at a wall when almost anybody in an overall and a cap could have done the assessment locally.

Our ringleader pleaded not guilty and demanded a proper court trial, bearing in mind that he did none of the painting and should not have been charged with the same crime as us. The response from the lady magistrate came as quickly as a thunderclap.

'Don't be so bloody stupid! You're guilty. You're all guilty!' and she promptly fined us.

In the general scheme of things, this was no big deal as nobody was hurt, nobody's life was ruined, but it did raise the question of how much justice was served that day, dished out by someone with a diametrically opposed political agenda to that of the defendants. Even if we had used eyebrow pencils for paint, the outcome would have been the same—guilty of malicious damage.

Ironically, our slogans were never removed but immediately painted over by the local fascist group. Most of the wall was then covered with Nazi slogans and exclamations of hatred for nearly everybody and everything: 'Down with ants.

They stink and steal our jobs!' Even the 'Bill Stickers will be Prosecuted' sign was painted over with something like, 'Leave him alone. He's one of us!' (Please excuse my literary licence, but I just couldn't resist it).

The best thing of all, to my mind, was that two of our group had succeeded in painting their slogans in large letters across most of the metal railway bridge by the station which crossed the main road through North Harrow to Rayner's Lane.

The following Easter, I got an after-school job pedalling a Wall's ice-cream tricycle around the deserted council estates of Acton Vale in a desperate attempt to make some money. What was more desperate was my flight from a marauding mob of six- to ten-year-olds who set about trying to steal the contents of the ice box.

The fully loaded tricycle was quite a thing to pedal, especially up an incline, but trying to pedal with eight or nine urchins clinging to the trike and round my neck and head was unbelievably difficult. Struggling to keep the lid to the icebox closed with one hand whilst warding off an assault with an outstretched foot, all the while pedalling and trying to keep in a straight line did have its funny side. I would have loved to have been a spectator.

I did two days of this toil, selling two or three ices the second day but decided that joining the Aldermaston March at Hounslow towards London would be more congenial.

Lunchtime at Kilburn Poly was more light-hearted in the company of a West African fellow I met. His family had sent him over to study, with future plans to return home, find a decent job, and help pay for another sibling to do the same.

My meagre monetary resources made it necessary for me to get as much food for as little money as possible. My lunch consisted of a currant loaf, which I bought from the local baker's shop for eleven pence. My African friend always bought bananas. On our first encounter one lunchtime, as I struggled through the dryness of the bread, he handed me a banana from his bag.

The next day, he again sat opposite me. This time, I decided to return the favour. I tore my loaf in half and passed it over, and once again, I received a banana. This went on for weeks, and during the lunch break, we were almost always together, sharing bread and bananas.

It didn't go down well with his fellow countrymen at all. They wouldn't speak to me, and because my friend liked to hold hands in true African kinship, as we went along the corridors one day, he was rebuked by one of them: 'He's not your brother. He's a white boy!'

He related a childhood episode in West Africa when he and a friend had gone out into the bush and found a huge bunch of bananas lying under a tree. They decided to carry it home between them, but it was so heavy, the only thing to do was to eat some of the fruit to make the bunch lighter. He said that there must have been well over one hundred-fifty bananas, and eating two or three didn't make it any lighter.

And so they ate more...and more...and more. They ate so many that they became very ill. 'They found us the next morning,' he said. 'We were oozing banana from every hole in our bodies, even our noses and ears, and it took us three weeks to recover.' He was off bananas for a long time after that.

Some members of the school did not appreciate the hand-holding, in particular, a tall boy who always appeared in cricket whites and who tried to ridicule me in front of his friends. I felt it necessary to let him know that I was not impressed with either his ignorance, size, or outfit. After all, he had inferred that I was homosexual with a particular racial preference, and I really could not let that pass. At the end of term, my friend returned to Africa, and that was the last I heard of him.

On almost every bank holiday, young people would hitchhike to the nearest coastal resort. One place in particular, Brighton, was a venue for large gatherings of beatniks. Late one Saturday night, I set off with a friend to join one such gathering. It was the first time I had hitchhiked. We arrived at our destination the following morning after travelling quite a long distance on foot.

A large gathering was already in evidence, grouped between the two piers and, apparently, under the leadership of the self-appointed 'King Fred'. I think he took himself a lot more seriously than anybody else did.

Once there, sitting on the shingle, I thought, What do we do now? I was half expecting that something exciting, an event perhaps, might take place. But no, we all just continued to chat quietly in the morning breeze. King Fred stood up and made a speech, which few of us could hear. It all seemed rather monotonous and boring.

I had been going out with a girl from Kilburn Poly for a while, and the relationship had soured through the malicious interference of a so-called friend, and so, we decided to split up.

We had both gone to a party the previous evening when my plan to go to Brighton later that night was revealed. The last time I had seen her before I left was with her shins poking out from under a table. She may have been examining the structural quality of the piece, but I somehow doubted it, believing that she was not alone. I was happy that she had found somebody to occupy her time.

To my great surprise, she appeared with her older sister, standing on the promenade overlooking the beach, searching among the many faces for one that she recognised. I ducked down and peered out to sea for half an hour, hardly daring to show my face. This was not what I wanted, and when I finally looked up, they had gone. It was sad in a way, but our relationship had really reached its end.

I got up and made my way to one of the local pubs with a couple of friends and met a barmaid from the Harrow area. The girl related how she had ended up working in the place. She had been desperate for money to buy food and had been told that there was work at the pub with accommodation. It sounded good, and she was offered the job and a bed.

The only problem was that the bed was the same one that the publican was using, and his expectations had to be met if she wanted to eat.

I was shocked. She was not much older than I but was enslaved and seemed to accept that this was all she could expect.

The day lingered on into the evening, and having drunk quite a lot, I was feeling quite cheerful. It was decided that our little gang would visit Applejohn's Cider Bar.

As we crossed the road from the promenade, a car stopped, and lo, there were my parents with my uncle John and his wife, Cath. They had come down to Brighton to seek me out, and I did not want that either. Let's face it—neither my mother nor father would want to be seen with me in Harrow because of my long hair. Yet there they were.

To make matters worse, my uncle with his Klaxon-like voice would be sure to attract half of Brighton's attention if he got a couple of drinks inside him. I waved and quickly disappeared into the throng.

At the end of the day, we started to look for shelter for the night, and the word spread that there was a derelict seafront hotel due for demolition which would be ideal. We all slipped in behind a corrugated iron barrier and carefully crept up the stairs and along corridors into the pitch blackness. Every room seemed to be full, and the smell of crumbling plaster and old urine, feline and human, pervaded the atmosphere.

Some had found broken furniture to burn in the fire-places, but most were content to just lie down and sleep.

And that is what we did until about 3am, when a burly voice boomed out across the room, 'Come on, you lot! Up you get! It's seven o'clock in the morning, and the sun's shining!'

Somebody asked if there was a cup of tea going, and the policeman replied that it was downstairs in the cafeteria. At least he had a sense of humour and had succeeded in getting all of us out into the dark street, still dazed from the evening before.

There were not a lot of options open at three in the morning, and the police made sure that nobody was going to get much sleep. There was no violence, just a lot of lost souls wandering about, and I think by morning, most of us were glad to get back on the road home.

By midday, having walked quite a long way from Brighton, two of us stood by the roadside trying to flag a ride. A car stopped nearby, and we thought it was a lift, so we hurried towards it. The occupants appeared a little surprised at our appearance, but realising we were hitchhikers, they welcomed us aboard.

They were two men and a woman, all middle-aged Caribbeans. They were headed to London, somewhere off Edgware Road. The woman chatted with us amicably, but before long, the car pulled off to the side of a petrol station and stopped. She fiddled around in her bag for a few seconds and produced a large kitchen knife. Turning to us, she said, 'Knife cut! Cut!'

I thought, Oh no, not again! But smiling, she got out of the car and set about cutting some flowers from the petrol station forecourt. One of the men had gotten out to buy some sweets. The other went for cigarettes as my friend and I sat motionless and slightly ill at ease.

Shortly, the three returned, the woman gushing over her flowers. The two men exchanged seats, and we resumed our journey. They stopped for another passenger who had crashed his motor bike. His arm was in a sling, and his t-shirt was still covered in his blood. He too sat in the back with us.

He was dropped off in South London, the smell of his blood leaving with him, and we continued across the city.

The driver had been somewhat erratic but nothing to worry about until we reached the Edgware Road, when a sharp left turn into a narrow street became necessary. It would have been fine if the Bentley hadn't been parked so close to the corner. We all sat dead still, staring in disbelief at the dent in the side of the limousine.

Suddenly, all doors flew open. The two men changed seats once more, bid us good luck as they shooed us away, and the car sped up the road and out of sight. We weren't far from Kilburn, and using my school train pass, I finally arrived home. Another weekend gone and still breathing!

As I said, everything was a jumble at this time. There were so many new people, new friends and parties.

A new kid arrived at Kilburn Poly, and he was unusual in that he had an affability and generosity not usual in Anglo-Saxons. This was probably because he was not an Anglo-Saxon but another Caribbean from Jamaica.

Being short of money for lunch as usual, I asked him if I could borrow a couple of bob until the following day. Instead, he took some pound notes from his wallet and popped one into my top pocket. I had always wanted to repay him, but he wouldn't let me. He said that he got enough money from dancing and gave me his card. It read 'Duncan Duncan', his stage name, but his real name was Carlton Duncan.

One of the best gatherings I ever attended was Carlton's birthday party, where I heard the music of Blue Beat records for the first time. Blue Beat was actually a record label which produced Jamaican R&B in the early sixties and was later considered to be synonymous with Ska, though the rhythms were quite different. To me, it will always be Blue Beat. That rhythm has echoed in my mind ever since.

At the party, he introduced me to Carmen, a lovely West Indian girl, but I had already drunk too much before I arrived to be of any company, and she soon found somebody else to socialise with.

Besides that, I was never able to dance. My feet always seemed to cement themselves to the floor. It was the fear of making a fool of myself, which I did regularly.

In the morning, as Carlton's dad shaved, the steady throb of the night's music started up once again, and I hung around as long as I could just to hear a bit more.

Carlton's star was slowly rising, and our paths led us in different directions, much to my regret.

Later in life, I found my old friend on a social media site and learned that he eventually became the first Black secondary school headmaster in Britain and an author. He has been a kind and loyal friend to this day.

22

A friend from Stanmore and I decided to hitchhike to Hastings one night for no memorable reason. We set off on foot from his house at about 9pm and headed south. By 11.30pm, we had reached Marble Arch, and as we continued on along the Vauxhall Bridge Road going towards Lewisham, we got a lift from a fairly unexpected quarter.

To give the man his due, he'd probably had a couple of drinks, and his judgement may have been slightly impaired when he decided to pick up a couple of beatniks, one of whom had a large Campaign for Nuclear Disarmament symbol painted on his duffel bag. I make this distinction because the driver was the Mayor of Deptford and Lewisham, and the act of picking up hitchhikers in an official car may have been viewed by some as compromising, especially he being a Tory.

He drove slowly and carefully through South London, pointing out various landmark buildings, until we reached Deptford. Then, driving even more slowly so that we could see the building better, he showed us the magnificent frontage of the town hall lit up by the streetlights, which he proudly declared was one of the finest examples in the south of London.

He dropped us off at Lewisham, bid us good luck, and cruised away, leaving us to continue our walk towards Bromley.

Our next lift was not immediate nor was it for any distance, only about three miles, but we had cleared the suburbs and were now on our way.

The distance between Bromley and Tonbridge is considerable, particularly on foot as we soon noticed. It was quite late at night, but to our surprise and relief, we managed to get a ride from Sevenoaks to Tonbridge. We carried on until we saw a group of hedges and trees in the moonlight. There, by the roadside, we decided to take a rest.

My companion, Dick Wardell, had a yellow AA guide to Britain sticking out of his bag, and at sunrise, staggering to our feet, we discerned that we were not alone. A horse had come to peer at us over a low gate, and seeing the nice yellow colour of the book, must have been convinced it would make enjoyable reading. Whipping it out of Dick's bag, the horse was about to make off with it when Dick realised what it was about to do.

Where it had learned to read, I'm not sure nor do I know who taught it, but the struggle that ensued had its funny side and left Dick with a book in a lot less pristine condition than it had been a few minutes before. The horse held the book firmly between his teeth and, wagging its head from side to side, gave Dick a good fight. Dick was not pleased, his book having suffered a serious nibble, but it was soon forgotten as we sauntered on towards Hastings.

When we reached Flimwell, we were picked up for the last part of the journey and were on the coast by 10am. It had taken thirteen hours to reach Hastings from Stanmore.

As we stood on Warrior Square in St. Leonards, Dick said that he fancied a cup of tea, and going to a phone box, he made a call. Not once had he mentioned his auntie on the way down. Thinking that we were both going to call in on her for tea, I was quite surprised by his sudden, 'See you later.'

He knew Hastings quite well, and I was under the impression that we were spending the weekend there together. Dick stayed with his auntie for three weeks, drank lots of tea, and not once did he show his face in the Hastings Old Town.

I returned by train to Charing Cross the next afternoon. I had eaten a bit, drunk a bit, met a few people, but I was definitely not going to try to hitch back to London, least of all on my own. I didn't see Dick again for several months, which was probably just as well. I did, however, continue to do a lot of walking, if only from one pub to another in various towns.

23

During the early part of 1959, my brother had picked up a plum job at Advance Laundry, where he slept most of the day and got paid top rate for the privilege. His two co-workers were Bernard Holley and a beat character named Arnold. He brought Arnold back home one night after he had been kicked out by his family. One night led to two, and two led to three months.

He slept in a sleeping bag on the floor of the living room, sang 'I Want to Ride in a Car, Car' at least three times a day, and sat up half the night writing poetry. His stay with us finally came to an end when he drank all of my mother's gin.

I don't think it was the missing gin so much as the fact that it was kept in my parents' bedroom. So he became a prowler and a drunkard in one move, which furnished the excuse to send him on his way.

I liked Arnold. He was quiet, unassuming, had an extraordinary accent, and was much better company than my brother ever was. I was sorry to see him go. He had managed to cap my mother's need to rage around the house with his very presence. She could not possibly risk being seen raving mad by an outsider and had to behave herself. I sometimes wondered if, when putting the washing on the line in the garden, she didn't sneak into the big black shed to have a screaming session in order to ease the tension that must have built up.

Arnold appeared on television the following year, along with Wiz Jones and a few beatnik friends in an Alan Whicker interview at Newquay. The local council had decided to wage war on the beatnik culture on account of their not being proper. The council denied them several human rights, including the rights to use public water, eat in a restaurant, work, and keep oneself clean. The council's behaviour begged the question: Who were the real freaks?

During the school summer holidays of 1960 and 1961, I had the indubitable privilege of working in the same sweat shop as my brother, Advance Laundry, under the pay grade of a 'girl under sixteen years of age'. This was an employment regulation set up to determine minimum wages by the Board of Trade, and it enabled companies to change a worker's age or gender in accordance with what work was available, although this was not the government's intention.

For example, an assistant to a woman on the pressing benches would be designated as 'girl's work' and would carry the lowest pay rate in the entire factory. The highest wages went to the drivers, and next down, to the loaders, who spent half their days sleeping, waiting for the vans to return from their pickups and deliveries later in the afternoons.

When I applied for work, Advance Laundry was the last resort, having been unable to find anything more suitable or interesting.

Around £4 a week and up to 4-10 shillings in the second year was the wage I earned for a forty-four-hour week with only forty minutes allowed for lunch and two ten-minute tea breaks per day. At least it stopped my mother from saying, 'You don't try hard enough', and though the money was also taxed, it was still more than I usually had.

The labour, in that respect, was worthwhile. Both years I was there, the factory machines were shut down and everybody had to stop work to listen to a pep talk from the managing director.

'I am sorry to tell you that owing to market conditions, we are having a bad time, and if you wish to keep your jobs, you must all work harder. I am not sure whether we can maintain the bonus rate that we pay you and are at present formulating...'

This speech would go on for half an hour, and I realised that it was just another means of squeezing even more blood out of these poor overworked stones. It was during this period that I came to despise capitalism and became interested in socialism in a purer form, especially after listening to that tripe. What was sadder was that some of the women took it on board, saying things like, 'Oh, he's so nice. We must try to help him.'

The outdoor summer heat and the hot steam from the rollers, wash boilers, and dryers were so intense, that working there was like being an ant in a furnace.

The first year was terrible, but the second year was not so bad. The women on the machines that rolled out the sheets wouldn't have me on their machines because I slowed them down too much, and they would lose some of their bonuses, which I wasn't entitled to anyway, so I was sent upstairs to help sort out the soiled linen as it came in from the hotels.

There, I was taken over to two young African women who were to explain to me what I had to do. Nothing odd in that, one would think, but these two were identical twins and both were rather plump, to put it mildly.

The fat that these two carried was not like real fat. They carried it as if it were just a mist or aura about them, so light that it could be dispersed with only the slightest breath. Their skin was smooth and their features fine and beautiful. I stood there mesmerised until, giggling like two school-girls, they each looped two fingers around one of my fingers on each hand and led me to a pile of hampers that had just arrived.

They spoke no English but exchanged a couple of phrases which were followed by more, somewhat saucy giggling. I am not going to elaborate on the fantasies that my adolescent mind conjured up, but suffice it to say they made my day.

Unfortunately, after a couple of hours, I was moved down to the dryers and was assigned to work under a woman of a different complexion. She was tall with a longish body and a dull, sad face. She looked at me with mild despair, probably convinced that I was not going to be of any assistance to her.

Before long, I realised that she was not well. She never ate and only drank a cup of tea during dinner break. I learned that she hardly ate at home either, living on a diet of tea and phenobarbital pills. She became less capable of work and noticeably weaker as the days went by. I took over her job but not her pay and continued to sweat in the overwhelming heat. Within a couple of weeks, she was gone.

It's funny, but whenever I ended up in a place surrounded by women, no matter how old they were, I was always viewed with suspicion. In this part of the laundry, it was no different.

It only lessened when one of the Caribbean men who did the heaviest work in the factory, was rebuked by his wife for glowering at me. He loaded the huge wash boilers with cartloads of already soaked linen, each cart weighing several hundredweight. He would methodically and slowly push each one up a ramp to the wash and then down again for the next load.

The ramp was in front of me, and behind me were banks of ironing boards with women doing the work, one of whom was his wife. Each time he passed in front of me, he'd scowl, and each time his wife would scold him, 'Leave him alone! He's only a boy!' or 'Don't! Stop that now!' in a lovely Trinidadian accent.

After about a week, he stopped. The ice was broken, and I was accepted into the throng. I found that they were a really nice group with a great sense of solidarity.

It was these women who, finding out how little I was being paid, complained to the management. No longer did I receive 'girl under sixteen' pay' but 'girl between sixteen and eighteen' wages. This was still less than the lowest male pay, and a lot less than a 'boy over sixteen' was being paid (he was actually younger than me), but it was only a holiday job and wasn't worth any more hassle.

There was an old Norfolk man who was employed, besides other things, to remove the stains which marred many of the sheets arriving from hotels. He looked like a wizard from a children's story, with a slightly hooked nose and extremely bushy eyebrows and ears, his skin deeply tanned and cracked from hours under an East Anglian sky. He smoked an old curly pipe and wore an ancient hat with a couple of tattered feathers in the band.

He was no less interesting than his appearance. After work, we often sat on his bench as he talked about the old times in Norfolk when he was a young man. He spoke of the magic recipes he used to remove the stains and of witchcraft and folklore that he had learned in his youth at the end of the nineteenth century. Once, he related how he and a friend had cast a spell using fresh spring water, sprinkling it in a circle under a full moon at the front gate of a farmer who had threatened them. The man trod in the circle the next morning and died within a few days.

The old man admitted that he was never sure if the death had anything to do with the spell or the incantation that he had uttered but regretted that he had gone so far to settle the dispute.

I would never want to work in a laundry again, but it was sad for the workers when the laundry eventually shut down, and they all lost their jobs. For some, it was their only liveli-hood, and for the Caribbean people, finding other employ-ment was likely going to be very difficult, prejudice being a fact of life in the greater Harrow area.

24

One of the great things about living in a small flat was that it was never far to the next room. Bumping into each other was a frequent occurrence. To avoid this, my father worked out a system whereby he could rest in complete peace under his car, or pretend to be busy in his shed.

My brother was a kind of hit-and-run merchant. His style was to use everything available in the kitchen, smear food and gravy up and down the walls, pretend to swoon over his creation, and in the blink of an eye, he would disappear. That left my mother, me, my cat Tibby, and Thumper the rabbit to get along the best we could.

My mother had taken poor old Thumper under her wing and gave him warm milk every night to cheer him up before he was put back into his hutch. Tibby and I tried to keep out of the way, but when things heated up, he too would jump out of my bedroom window and have a poo in the upstairs neighbour's coal bin. That left my mother and me.

When my father was around the house in the evening, he would stuff as much into his stomach as it would hold and then dissolve into the arms of Morpheus, only to leap out of his chair after half an hour or more with a cramp in his leg. That quelled, he'd take his Rennies to cure his indigestion, then smoke his pipe. He loved to think that he was living the high life by gormandising on Gentleman's Relish, which was really just another fish paste, or Cracker Barrel cheese, which usually caused my tongue to break out in blisters.

'You can't beat a good bit of Cracker Barrel!' was his usual comment as he stuffed another two or three Rennies into his mouth.

If this behaviour was upsetting to my mother, I wouldn't know because she would continue to pander to him. 'Do you want some more Cracker Barrel, Cyril, or would you like Gentleman's Relish? How many crackers would you like?' And that was usually less than an hour after having eaten a full evening meal.

It was the Rennies that finally got him and not my mother. He was dragged off to hospital to have his gallbladder removed. After the operation, the surgeon informed him that it was crammed full of chalk. 'Oh, that might be the Rennies,' was my dad's sheepish response.

My mother would usually wait until he had finished eating and his cramp was quelled before she'd prick him with, 'Why is it that George and Iris have got more money than we have? After all, she doesn't even have to work, and you say that you and George get the same wages.'

My father was not going to admit he'd spent most of it playing around with the car. 'I don't know. I can't understand it,' he said, which was not the answer she wanted. From then on, he was in for it. I would retire to my bedroom with Tibby and try to get him to do my homework for me.

The temperature in the living room would rise, and my mother would eventually storm off to bed with my father whimpering, 'Joanie, oh Joanie,' whilst holding a cup of Ovaltine in one hand and a fag in the other. It was usually more peaceful when he wasn't there, but Tibby was always cautious and chose to lay on my bed just in case.

One late afternoon, on arriving back at the flat, I found my brother in the last throes of daubing the walls in the kitchen with gravy and slopping all sorts of culinary offal over the top of the gas cooker. He settled down in front of his plate, not unlike a pig at a trough. With his nose twitching with excitement, he wolfed the lot down with plenty of self-congratulatory moans and a couple of glasses of wine in a matter of minutes. Then throwing his plate into the sink along with every saucepan that my mother owned, he turned and went out.

As luck would have it, my mother came back from work a few minutes later, and on seeing the mess in the kitchen, justly freaked out. Personally, I would have done the same. The one difference was that I would have targeted the actual perpetrator. Unfortunately, this was not the way my mother's mind worked. Tibby, on seeing what was coming, left the kitchen and hid under the big black shed at the bottom of the garden, leaving me to meet the onslaught head on.

'How dare you leave the kitchen in such a mess when you know I've done a hard day's work. I don't care if it was his fault,' and so it went. There was nothing I could say that she'd either hear or want to hear, so I did the washing up just to keep the peace.

When my brother had reached the age of sixteen a few years before, my parents gave him an envelope containing a little bundle of five-pound notes, twelve in all. Knowing that this was from the maturity of an insurance policy, I assumed that I would receive the same amount a few years later, when it became my turn.

When I reached sixteen, nothing happened. I thought there was some mistake and eventually asked my parents about it.

My father said, 'You've already had it!' which surprised me because I felt sure I would have remembered holding the little bundle, even if just for a few minutes. But I didn't, and I started to wonder what it was that I had received and not known about.

I thought for a while about past events and recalled a phrase uttered by my father when our old black and white television finally went caput. He and my mother were discussing how to find the money for a new set, and my father muttered under his breath, 'There's always Barry's money.'

I remember thinking, *What is Barry's money? Barry doesn't have money,* and I let it pass. It was then I recalled that the insurance man used to turn up at about one o'clock, just in time for egg and chips. But not anymore, not for quite a few years.

I made the connection and realised that there was a cost to watching Felix the Cat, Popeye, and The Quatermass Experiment. It was sixty pounds, and there was no way that I was ever going to get it. I knew that I would never get the money or a straight answer, so I just let it go.

It was at this time that I should have left home, but unfortunately, I didn't, and I allowed myself to fester in a household where I was given about the same respect as Tibby, and that wasn't much. Besides, where would I go at sixteen, and how would I live?

My parents loved Christmas. It was a time for my mother to sparkle and for my father to adopt Stewart Granger poses. People commented on the similarity between the two men, and it was upsetting and sad to think that there were so many who had such serious visual problems.

It was always cold, nothing to do, nowhere to go, and the Christmas of 1961 was no exception. I had gone out for a walk in the morning to get out of the flat. Not finding any other lost souls roaming the streets, I returned at about 2pm only to find the flat empty.

I waited till mid-afternoon before going out once more, having noticed that nothing had been prepared for dinner, which struck me as being odd. Tibby had got fed up and gone off to bed, leaving his paper party hat by the side of his bowl. I thought that he probably had the right idea, but I couldn't help wondering where my parents had gone. I wandered around the park until dark and returned once more to the empty flat.

At about seven that evening, I thought I would go round to a friend's house just around the corner when my father's car finally appeared. My father was alone and seemed a little spaced out but tried to make out that it was me who had been missing.

"We're all round at the Hughes' house,' he said, as if I should have known.

I had gone to primary school with Michael Hughes but hadn't seen him for five years. His sister, Pat, had at one time gone out with my brother. Now my mother, always wanting to live in my brother's sunshine, had somehow made the acquaintance of her parents. I didn't really want to get involved, but my father persuaded me to go back with him.

It was party time! My mother had been drinking Baby-cham since 11am and had actually got tipsy on it. Deter-mined to show how with it she was, she grabbed hold of my wrists and demanded that I jive with her, pulling my arms first one way and then the other. As usual, my feet stuck firmly to the floor. What ensued was an embarrassing show of maternal coercion for cheap laughs as she shook me about like a rag for at least five minutes before she realised that I was not dancing.

It all became too much for her, and she staggered out to the loo to be sick. It was a good time to leave and let the Hughes family have what remained of their day to them-selves.

Needless to say, she didn't feel too much like eating and went straight to bed when we got home. My father had eaten his way through countless turkey sandwiches, so he wasn't hungry. My brother, who was in Paris at that time, would not have been hungry either, guaranteed.

So, it was left to me to sort something out for myself. This, in itself, was not a hardship, but it would have been good to have known earlier that a proper Christmas dinner was not on the menu. I had been hungry for much of that day, but by the end of it, I had lost my appetite. I made myself an omelette and was soon off to bed. I found Tibby between the sheets with his head on my pillow. What solace!

25

The last few months of my sixteenth year were quite boring, apart from being shot in my left nipple by a boy with an air pistol who thought I might make a good target. Actually, it was quite painful and made my eyes water a little. The last time I had been hit that hard was when Micky Rolfe caught me dead in the centre of my forehead with a stone from his catapult. It was a parting shot, and I didn't see him again for several years. That made my eyes water too.

I had been hitching to Hastings quite regularly over the summer holiday, and having made a few friends there, it was not hard to find accommodations for the night on Don Hirst's floor.

The house was in the throes of renovation, so it didn't matter that Don's room was taken over by sleeping dogs at night as long as they didn't bark too much.

On one occasion, I had arranged with a quiet young guy from Harrow Art School, Henry W., to make the trip. He was, he said, being messed around by his girlfriend and thought that by exhibiting some independence, it would show her—what, I don't know. We reached Hastings in record time, and at the end of the evening, we went back with Don to his house.

There was a glimmer of trouble brewing, emanating like thin steam from the top of Henry W.'s head, and before long, he started to verbally abuse our host. I thought that Henry was a gentle sort of person, but as he started to threaten Don, I felt it necessary to change my mind. Don tried to keep things on an even keel and suggested that Henry should calm down and go to sleep. It didn't seem much of a red rag to me, but obviously Henry took it badly and threw himself on top of Don with the intent to cause him some major injury.

Henry was larger than Don, but the fight ended after fifteen minutes, with Henry the loser but still persistently abusive. He was told to shut up or get out, and grudgingly, he did the former.

The following day, we returned to the road and got stuck outside Sidcup railway station. After a short period of cussing, Henry produced a large knife from his duffel bag and started waving it around and foul mouthing the passing cars. We didn't have a clue where Sidcup was, and Henry refused to walk any further. To me, he appeared to be losing it, whatever 'it' was.

I thought that a call to my father might save the day. I really didn't want to get arrested for being with this big clod. Reluctantly, I made the call, reversing the charge, and asked my father for a lift. Needless to say, my father could hardly believe his luck. Being out of the flat during my mother's Sunday afternoon ironing rant fest and having the chance to drive his beloved banger was just what he needed. He was with us in a surprisingly short time.

On returning to North Harrow, we dropped Henry off, and I didn't see him again, nor did I want to. The next time I saw Don, he said that he didn't mind me going back to his place as long as there was no one else with me, which I thought was very reasonable.

There was a good folk/blues element at The Anchor on George Street in Hastings, and if one wanted a great evening, drinking in a smoky, noisy, and friendly pub, that was the place to be.

One Saturday evening, the fun was in full swing with an impromptu string and jug band and myself hooting and *wa-wa*-ing into a beer glass with a kazoo. The cigarette I had been smoking was still in my left hand, sticking outwards between my third and fourth fingers. In my exuberance, I accidentally poked it straight into my left eye.

The pain was excruciating. Don and David got me to the local A & E, where a nurse cleaned out the debris and a doctor prescribed some eye drops. We had to wait quite a while for the medicine and finally left just before the pub's closing time. That was unfortunate because none of us had any more than a pint all evening.

We all ended up in the coffee bar across the road from the pub and ordered our coffees. I was losing my co-ordination, and suddenly, I blacked out. I stood up knocking the table over and marched out of the bar like a zombie in a mist. Somehow, I made it through the alleyways that led to the seafront, across the main road, and onto the beach, where I collapsed onto the gravel. I was not consciously aware of my movements.

Don found me about half an hour later and led me back to his place to sleep. I cannot explain why I had blacked out, though I think it was the pain, but again, I had walked without any conscious vision for at least two-hundred yards without falling over anything.

After three weeks, my vision was still no better, and I thought I should go to my own doctor. She thought that there was something amiss and asked me to go back home and collect the eye drops that came from the hospital. I returned later that evening, and peeling back the dosage labels which covered the medicine details, she discovered that the hospital had reversed the dosage. I had been taking one drop three times a day instead of once and the second drops once instead of three times a day.

In a week, my eye was better, and the fog had cleared. Smoking is definitely bad for one's health in more ways than one imagines.

Returning to Kilburn Poly was almost a relief after the summer chaos, but it was not long before another bout of tonsillitis grabbed me by the throat. After spending another few days at home, I was glad to get back into the swing of things, but on reaching Wembley Park station, all of that suddenly changed.

I met up with Bernard, his girlfriend, Jill, and Dick B. from school, who were waiting for Dick's girlfriend to arrive. As her train pulled away from the opposite platform, she stood there for an instant, looking for her friends.

I had only ever seen one girl who I could say was unbelievably beautiful, and that was Shirley. I knew absolutely nothing about Shirley, I might add. But suddenly, there across the track was another absolutely stunning girl. I was totally overwhelmed.

Bernard and Dick had taken the day off from school to accompany the girls to the V&A Museum where they were going to study. I thought that having already lost three days, another wouldn't matter too much and tagged along with them. It was very difficult trying to be at ease among the others with my nose perpetually choked up and the raucous cough barking every few seconds. I was sure that I wasn't making too much of an impression on this divinity either.

We changed trains at Baker Street, and then it happened. My nose began to bleed profusely. I always carried three or four handkerchiefs in my pocket when I had a cold, but they were soon saturated. Reaching South Kensington, I slipped into a shop to buy some more. Still the blood came, and reluctantly, the shop staff allowed me to rinse my face, hands, and the bloody handkerchiefs in their washroom.

At the V&A, the blood was still pouring, and having left a small puddle on the floor of the lift, I finally went to their first-aid room where I laid down for half an hour.

It eventually stopped, and being now quite lightheaded, I rejoined the others in the tearoom, feeling even more of a disaster than I did in the beginning.

I have always blamed Cynthia for that event. She was just too beautiful for my fragile constitution to cope with.

We all had something to eat, but feeling that my nose had grown to colossal proportions, it was a most uncomfortable, embarrassing situation. She sat across the table, and though I couldn't take my eyes off her, I was incapable of acting coherently. It wasn't until later that I learned she had been the hot-headed nutter, Henry's girl. I did see her again, much to Dick's distress. He had been swooning over her for days, and I really felt quite bad about replacing him. But it soon passed, as things do.

For my birthday, she bought me a really nice V-neck jumper. My mother was furious. She had been undermined by another female and was not at all happy. For once, she nearly managed to keep her anger under wraps but could not quite stop herself from casting a sharp glance at Cynthia when I unwrapped the gift.

That Christmas, I worked at the post-office sorting workroom in Harrow. Because I wouldn't be paid until at least ten days after I had finished, I asked my father to loan me a few pounds to buy Cynthia a present. He refused. My mother also refused, saying, 'Ask your father.' I couldn't find a way to raise some cash. I was sure it was refused out of spite and aimed at weakening our relationship.

I blew it anyway a couple of months later when I got drunk at a party in Hampstead and was carried away bodily by a group of people, most of whom I didn't really know. Some of them ended up on the living room floor of my parents' flat for the night. I had left with Cynthia's purse in my pocket, leaving her stranded at the party, and though I had no intention of leaving without her, the events all seemed a little too engineered to be accidental.

My removal was done so quickly that Cynthia had no idea I was gone, and nobody had informed her. The fact that I was carried out when I could have walked was also a little strange. I did drink too much, and it was all my fault, so I had no one to blame but myself.

The whole weekend was bent on becoming a nightmare. On arriving at my parents' flat, I asked one of the group, Dick Wardell (now known as Kid Wardell, the blues singer) to light the bathroom stove. It was a paraffin convector heater with a little metal chimney over the burner, and if the chimney was not turned on correctly, the stove would smoke, which is precisely what happened.

Everybody had flaked out on the floor, and being the first to wake in the morning, I thought that I was seeing things. All six of us had turned black overnight, each of us coated liberally with soot, as was everything in the bathroom, the kitchen, and the living room. To round it off, all the clean washing that my mother had left in the bathroom was evenly covered in ash residue. For a moment, I wondered where they had all come from. It was a bit like a comedy but without the laughs.

My parents had been away for the weekend but were due back that evening. We all set to work washing the walls, the cooker, the cupboards, and I rewashed all of my mother's stuff. The end result didn't look too bad. By the end of the afternoon, only Dick remained. None of us had stopped for anything to eat, but as the others disappeared one by one, I was eventually left on my own.

When my parents arrived, I explained what had happened in the flat in a roundabout way. At first, it appeared to be accepted with the promise that I would have another go at cleaning the following day.

It was okay for five minutes, but then my mother went to the kitchen cupboard drawer, took out a carving knife, threw herself on the floor, and started to scream, 'I'm going to kill myself!' With her legs kicking up in the air, the knife whirling round and round, and all the shrieking, I would not have been surprised if she had cut her arm off. But she didn't.

My father cried out, 'Joanie, oh, Joanie! Don't do it. Don't do it!' and I walked out. My mother would not have hurt herself, not intentionally. Self-love does not allow that sort of thing to happen.

The following Tuesday, I handed Cynthia's purse back to her at Willesden Green station, and there, she finished our relationship. She turned her back and walked away along the platform, and I knew I would never see her again.

When I got home, Tibby was waiting for me on the couch. I flopped down beside him, and putting his paw on my arm, he said, 'Yes, I liked her too.'

26

After Cynthia and I split up, I returned to the West End on weekends and usually got a little tipsy and less inhibited than I would normally be. I don't remember too much about it all except for the samplings of Guinness and bitter at more than one pub.

One of the things I do remember was leaving The Blue Posts on Berwick Street. Something had amused me to such an extent that I fell over laughing, and falling over made me laugh even more. As I lay on the pavement incapable of controlling my mirth, a large black limousine pulled up beside me. The door opened, and a beautiful woman looked down at me. A manicured hand wearing a large ring reached out and touched my face.

'Aw, he's so lovely,' she said. 'Can't we take him home?' which was quickly followed by a gruff, 'No!'

She was pulled back inside the car, the door slammed, and the apparition disappeared. It brought me back to my senses, as such things would, and I wandered off in the direction of the station to go home. I have always fostered the illusion that she was the beautiful English teacher from Kil-

burn Poly, and if she had been, I would have loved to go off
with her in that car.

Another evening, I came across my brother in the street.
I was looking for a loo, and obligingly, he said that there was
one nearby. He took me inside the doorway of a house and
said, 'This place belongs to a friend of mine. I use it all the
time. The loo's just there on the landing.'

Sure enough, there was the lavatory just as he had said.
He was hanging about at the bottom of the stairs when the
front door opened, and a burly guy came into the hallway.

'Who the hell are you? What are you doing here?' thun-
dered the behemoth. 'Get out and don't let me catch you
here again!'

It was a sticky moment, and we were both lucky to have
gotten away in one piece.

'I thought you said that it belonged to a friend of yours!'

It just so happened to be the entrance to a small brothel,
and the big guy was there to look after things. I should have
known not to ask my brother for anything, least of all a public toilet.

Most of the time, I was immured at the Duke of York,
but as it became more and more crowded, most of the people that I knew ended up at Finches on Goodge Street. It
was a bigger pub, and there was a good chance of being able
to find a seat. It didn't have the cachet of the Duke of York,
but most of the old timers eventually moved in

My brother decided to give up on London and packed his
bags for Paris. He called most of his old friends and asked

to meet up at the Champion for a farewell party at his expense. He even invited me and said that he would be there at around 8.30pm.

Between sixteen and twenty friends showed up. We waited...and waited. Having learnt my lesson, I bought my own drinks, and a few of the others did the same. Some chose to wait.

At about fifteen minutes before the pub was to close, the door opened and in sauntered my brother, flanked on either side by what looked like two bouncers. He delivered a farewell speech that even Papa Doc would not have dared to pronounce. Basically, he poured verbal excrement over everybody who had waited for him for being leeches and nobodies, people with no futures and total failures.

The heavies stood beside him, apparently unmoved. That they might have understood what he had said was doubtful, and how he came to be in such company begged a follow-up question. By the time he had finished, the pub closed, and he had succeeded in wasting several hours of other people's lives, not surprisingly, since it had become a regular habit of his.

During that period, my mother had honed her skill at prying into other people's lives, notably those of my brother and me. Mine was quite well hidden and not really interesting to her. However, my brother had begun writing two massive journals filled with accounts of his shenanigans, which my mother was eager to read. This included passages of a sexual nature. If he brought any girl home for the night, my mother would fuss around the poor thing in the morning, trying to glean as much information as possible, including what their future plans were.

Sometimes, if I came home really late, it was not uncommon to find somebody in my bed, and I would have to sleep in the living room for the night. She regularly searched our bedroom, pawing through everything in our drawers. Visitors needed to look out also. An unguarded handbag could be rifled through, and even if she were caught on the job, as Cynthia had once noted, she would make some feeble excuse and brush it off without an apology. Some of my meagre possessions would sometimes mysteriously disappear, particularly my clothes.

The diary reading became more obsessive, and I would find her at least twice a week with her head buried deep in the pages.

After my brother left for Paris, she and my father started to go out at least three times a week. It was good because they were out of my hair. It gave my mother the chance to sparkle again and my father a renewed opportunity to feel important as 'Big Cyril'. My mother's dips into madness subsided. There were other people to be interfered with.

She didn't have to look far for a victim. Connie Thomas, our next-door neighbour, was a district nurse. As if things couldn't get any worse, she also owned a car. To cap it all off, the car had 'District Nurse' and other medical highfalutin titles plastered on the side door, which was enough to stir a nuclear explosion. Every day seemed to be spent looking out the front window to watch Connie's comings and goings.

Mother would exclaim, 'She can't drive that car! I should be doing that!' or 'I'd hate to be nursed by her, stupid woman!' or 'Look at her. She can't even reverse! I don't think she knows which is the front and which is the back of the car!'

When Connie was off work and in the back garden, she sometimes took her secateurs to a small pear tree, which was not a happy little tree. It was nobody's business how mutilated the poor thing was, but my mother always made a thing of it.

'Look what she's done. She wouldn't know a root from a branch! Hope she cuts her fingers off. That will teach her, the stupid bitch!'

This had been building up for some time, and it was solely a one-sided affair. The fact that Connie was a woman, a professional woman at that, was akin to being the monster from the black lagoon, but the car was the real catalyst.

My mother had passed her driving test before the war but was not really cut out to drive on a road—on a field maybe, but not on a public highway. In her mind, she was the only woman in the world who had the right to drive, and seeing Connie behind the wheel was just too much for her.

One evening, Connie's husband came to the door, and after talking to my mother for a short while, he made the error of saying, 'Grow up, Joan! Grow up!'

Big mistake. He had just tread on a viper's tail. Enraged, my mother summoned the aid of my father, who took it upon himself to hit Tommy, sending him sprawling backwards over a low wall between the two front doors.

That was the second member of their family who had been hit by one of ours. I had socked their Scotty dog in the jaw after it had sunk its teeth into my ankle, but I think that was a lot more justified than my father's action. For a few days after, I hoped my parents would be picked up for assault, but it didn't happen. I hasten to add that my father's position at Walter Kiddie was solely due to Tommy's goodwill. Some gratitude!

One night, while my father was away, my mother and I were visited by a thief on a bicycle. He brought it down the front path and leaned it against my parents' bedroom wall. He then proceeded to creep around the side of the house, past my bedroom window.

That was not our first burglar. At a time when my memory was unrelated to salient events, I awoke one morning to find an old army sock hanging from the stay that held the little top window open in my bedroom. I remember seeing it, but I was too little to understand its significance. But to my parents, it was obvious that someone had tried to enter through that window, using the sock as a cushion to prevent getting gashed by the window's stay.

The present burglar was different because this time, I saw him. I had just gotten into the top bunk bed and turned out the light. I rarely bothered to close the curtains since it only served to make the room look smaller than it really was. I happened to be sitting up when the intruder passed by. At first, neither of us registered the presence of the other, it being dark on both sides of the glass, until we realised we were looking straight into each other's eyes.

As he turned to run, I jumped out of bed. He made for his bike, and I went for my trousers. He got his transport stuck in the front gate, and I grabbed the carving knife from the kitchen drawer. On my way to the front door, my mother, having heard the commotion and cussing of our visitor, bumped into me in the hallway, and seeing the knife in my hand, she blocked my way.

'He'll have that off you in a trice and stick it in you, and then where will you be!' she said, and with that, she snatched the blade away from my hand. True to form, she replaced it with a broom.

By this time, the burglar was well on his way, his bike creaking with strain from every thrust on the pedals. I was on his case and halfway across the gravel road when I realised I was barefoot. This was quite an impediment. It was about a quarter to midnight, and there was no one around to assist as I hobbled after him, half running and half hopping. He was already fifty yards ahead on the road to Wealdstone when I eventually gave up the chase. I satisfied myself by shouting abuse at him.

'You bastard! If I see you up here again, you've had it! I'll slam you with my broom, so you better watch out!' I then turned and went back to bed.

27

Camber Sands on the eastern side of Rye Harbour in East Sussex was hardly the place to start a story about Paris or, for that matter, about Strasbourg. What the experience did was demonstrate how totally unrelated events can change the course of one's life and why sometimes the path not chosen might have been a better choice than the one followed.

My next-door neighbour, David, and I had gone to Hastings for the weekend, and having heard about a beach party at Camber that Saturday evening in 1962, we decided to go there after the pubs had closed. Apparently, the police had shut the event down almost as soon as it had started, and when we arrived, the beach was deserted.

Camber Sands is a huge, flat sand beach which, when the tide is out, stretches for several hundred yards to meet the retiring sea. On this calm moonlit night, the tide had just started to trickle back in across the sand, and on the crest of each ripple, millions of phosphorescent algae danced as if the sea were enchanted. As far as one could see, the water was alight, flickering and rolling out towards the horizon. It was absolutely amazing, and I have never had the pleasure to have seen anything like it since.

We passed the night in the sand dunes, and in the morning, wandered off to get a cup of tea from the café by the car park. The café was closed, but as we passed a large, parked truck, we noticed some movement under the tarpaulin that covered its back.

First one head appeared and then another close by, the second one sinking back down again, out of sight. A third head appeared at the other end of the truck. The first face was that of 'Moor Park Jane', a very attractive, very sexy and somewhat wild twenty-year-old who I knew quite well from around North Harrow and Pinner. The second was that of the lorry driver, and the third at the other end was Genevieve, a really good-looking French student who was staying with Jane's family in Moor Park.

I was seventeen, and my mother had arranged with my brother, odd as it may seem, for me to spend a couple of weeks during the summer with him in Paris. At the time, he was teaching English at the Berlitz Language School on Boulevard des Italiens, a job that he acquired by claiming, among other things, that he had been an assistant lecturer of philosophy at Chiswick Polytechnic.

Boarding the cross-channel ferry with an old soft suitcase, a duffle bag, and my guitar, I headed straight for the bar and settled down uncomfortably alone to watch the comings and goings of the other passengers. As the ferry approached the French coast, I came face to face with Genevieve,

'Where are you going?' she asked.

'Paris.'

'You're mad!' she said. 'I'm going home to Strasbourg. Come with me. You can stay at our house. My father is a doctor, and he would be happy that you are there to teach me English, and you can stay as long as you like as our guest.'

Wow! I thought, and she was correct. I was mad. Not wanting to let my brother down, I politely declined and caught the train to Paris. And there ended the connection with Camber Sands and Genevieve.

What a shame that when these sorts of choices present themselves, one cannot sample them first before making a decision. I could have gone off with her to Strasbourg, shed the links with my family, and learned to speak French. When faced with a choice, we often take the road we know rather than brave the uncertainty of the unknown, and so my life's little chaos continued to whirl.

I eventually reached Paris and was totally lost. My immediate response was to go to the nearest bar in the train station and order a glass of Beaujolais. I had no francs and tried to pay for the wine with half a crown. The waitress looked at the coin, then at me, and pointing to the *bureau de change* across the station, sent me on my way.

Having changed my cash, I returned to the bar to pay for the wine. The waitress had already forgotten who I was, and misunderstanding what I was trying to say, she gave me another glass of Beaujolais. Nobody had mentioned to me anything about the little red Bakelite dish that came with every glass. No, it wasn't a coaster but served as one very nicely.

On finishing this second glass, I offered the waitress some money. She pointed to the little red tray which I promptly gave back to her with the empty glass. She raised her eyes to heaven and gestured for me to go. I don't know what 'bugger off' is in French, but I think that was what she was trying to say.

Anyway, two free glasses of Beaujolais weren't bad for a start. Now it was time to tackle the Metro. The system is quite easy provided you know how to use it. It was only by stopping people and asking them if they spoke English that a German couple eventually gave me directions to l'Opera. From there, getting to Boulevard des Italiens was simple, and after walking for ten minutes, I thought I'd better enquire the whereabouts of the Berlitz Café.

Seeing two gendarmes standing outside a cinema, I seized the opportunity and asked for directions. They discussed the situation for some minutes between themselves, one pointing in one direction and the other shaking his head and pointing in the opposite direction. This went on for quite a while, and I began to feel a little uneasy and thought that maybe I was on the wrong street. Finally, both of them pointed to their right, and there was the café. I had been standing in front of it all along. They looked at me very sternly, turned their backs, and sauntered off down the busy street.

It was about 2.30pm when I entered the bar and, again not knowing the rules regarding cafés, I ordered a coffee at the bar then sat at a table. Wrong move. Apparently, when ordering a coffee at the bar, one had to stand there and drink it. If sitting at a table, one had to wait for the waiter to order and be served. I was asked, in a very curt manner, to stand up and have my coffee at the bar. I assumed that the tables were not for the likes of me or they were all reserved.

My brother was to meet me around four o'clock. As he was working just above the café, one would have thought it wouldn't be too difficult to keep the appointment. But four o'clock passed as did five o'clock and six o'clock, by which time my legs were beginning to buckle.

The man behind the bar realised that I didn't have a clue about the *système* and told me to sit down. I had already drunk several cups of coffee, some cognac, and a beer just for something to do. Finally, at six-thirty, my brother deigned to make an appearance. It was only when the bar-man saw him flit by and called after him that he rushed over to speak to me.

'Oh!' he said. 'Can't stop. I've got a lesson now. I'll see you at eight-thirty,' and off he went again.

I should have known better than to believe him. I hadn't had anything to eat since I'd left North Harrow except for a couple of sandwiches in my bag. I was starving, and the idea of waiting another two hours was infuriating. I couldn't see any food in the café, and I didn't know how to ask anyway. There were probably baguettes and salad and cheese, but it was all behind the bar and out of sight. So I waited until, at last, my brother returned.

He lived in a bedsit off Avenue de Messine, just behind the Jacquemart-André Museum, not that he ever mentioned that, and after having a stand-up meal in a bar, we walked the two kilometres to his place. He introduced me to the concièrge at the door, and in we went.

There was no hot water in the place and no food was to be eaten in the room either, but that rule was, by necessity, broken every day. I believe most tenants had a little Primus stove tucked away to heat water for washing or to make coffee. I slept on the floor under a clothes rack. Truth be told, I was so tired, I would have slept on razor blades and tin tacks.

In the morning, I awoke just in time for him to give me directions back to Paris centre before he returned to the school. I thought that it might be a good idea to use the Berlitz Café as a base and wander around from there.

It was August and intensely hot, so I sat outside the café and watched the comings and goings of the passersby. A woman in her late fifties had walked past a short while before, and on returning, she stopped in front of me. From the little French that I knew, I gathered that she was asking me to go with her to her flat, that we could dance together, and because I looked tired, I could go to sleep. I don't know if I got it right, but she was quite adamant and took hold of my hand.

Thinking, *What do I do now?* I hastily replied, *'J'attends mon frère'* (I'm waiting for my brother), but she was having none of that. With a sudden jerk, she had me off my seat and started to literally drag me down the street. My brother later said I should have gone with her.

'It might have been a good experience,' he said, but I didn't think I was quite ready to find that out. I struggled free from her and returned to my seat. I saw her pass regularly with other male companions around her age or older, with her nose in the air.

To give my brother some credit, he did take me to a few eateries, a couple of clubs, and there I met several people with whom I spent most of my time.

One morning, he said, 'We'll have lunch here today, so buy some eggs, a baguette and a tin of pipenade.' French is a very concise language, and if you didn't get it right the first time, they wouldn't understand or even try to guess what you wanted.

The first linguistic hurdle was asking for eggs. To pronounce it properly, one egg is *erf* and ten eggs are *oo*, but you can't have ten *erfs*. It took me ten minutes of hen-speak and playing charades with the exasperated shopkeeper before he got it. He didn't smile throughout the entire performance.

Then there was the 'pepinade'—no such thing. It was, in fact, 'piperade', only one letter off and the rest slightly jumbled but enough to confuse a dozen shopkeepers. Eventually, the problem was solved at a very expensive shop in the centre of Paris, with the tin costing three or four times the usual price.

We ate French bread, scrambled eggs, and piperade for lunch. In the evening, we ate out with my brother's girlfriend at a Japanese restaurant, then went to Le Bal Nègre. The latter was a dance hall where elderly white ladies would go to dance with young Black men. The band, a quartet led by a saxophonist, played a tired, half-hearted jazz, worn out by weeks of repetition.

Money obviously changed hands there since it was, for some of the men, their only source of income. It had a sad, sleazy atmosphere about it, a far cry from the seedy but energetic holes-in-the-wall back home.

I was the only young, unattached white male in the place, and it was not long before I felt a hand on my shoulder. Looking up, I peered into the questioning eyes of a woman in her late sixties. I declined her request and sat rigid without daring to look up again should somebody else approach me.

It was crazy, really. In England, it wouldn't have bothered me too much, but not being able to understand the language put a different slant on the situation as I sat there sweating in the hot, smoky room. I would have loved to relax more and enjoy the scene, but, unfortunately, tension was such a close companion for most of my stay in Paris. and this was certainly no exception.

On another evening, we ate at a Yugoslav restaurant, and right from the start, things began to happen. The walls moved!

It was a dimly lit place, but quite well set out. The wallpaper was striped vertically, and between each line were small decorative elements, rather like fleur-de-lis appliques. Out of the corner of my eye, I thought I saw one of these objects move towards another. The more I looked, the more they moved, until eventually the whole wall seemed to be alive—which indeed it was!

I can't tell you how many roaches there were, but it was easily in the hundreds. My brother explained, 'You know, they're part of the restaurant staff and clean the floor during the night. They also don't need to be paid, and since they don't bite, they're welcomed in any restaurant.'

One might be forgiven for thinking that my brother had a good sense of humour, but it wasn't so much humour as it was an actual belief, strange as it seemed. It was much like his conviction that 'calves have to be taken from their mothers; otherwise, they will suckle until they burst.'

Since the cockroaches didn't seem to bother anybody else in the restaurant, I carried on eating the bread and drinking the wine until our dinner arrived.

As the evening wore on, there was a tap, tap, tap at the door, and when the woman proprietor opened it, the grizzled shape of an old tramp holding out a wooden bowl appeared. She took the bowl into the kitchen, filled it with bits and pieces along with half a baguette, and handed it back to him.

Not long after, there was another tap, tap, tap at the door, but this time, the door opened, and an arm with the bowl at the end of it oozed its way into view. The proprietor snatched the bowl from the hand, swung the door wide open, and cracked the unfortunate over the head with it. As he retreated, she flung the bowl after him. I had a notion that this was a regular performance.

One of the other teachers at the Berlitz School was an old eccentric by the name of Ross. His whole way of life seemed to be somewhat off-target, and one might say that, in some ways, he appeared to have just landed.

Late one evening, my brother took us around the St. Denis market and through the area frequented by prostitutes. Ross walked up and down in front of the girls, and in the half light, peered into some of their faces, stood back, looked them up and down, more in the manner of study rather than sexual intimidation. He hummed and aha'd as if he were learning something, then walked on as if they didn't exist.

Later that night, he opened his wallet and produced a Durex packet with the top torn open, and asked me, 'Can I still use this? I opened it some months ago. Do you think it might have perished?'

Not being an expert on the matter, I told him to ask my brother, which he probably did. Whether or not he ever got round to using it was highly doubtful.

On another evening, at an Asian restaurant which only had curried chicken on the menu, he asked the waiter for chicken without the curry. An argument ensued because he didn't want to pay for the curry, only for the chicken. What made matters worse, the waiter wore a turban, which Ross took to mean that the man was Indian and, therefore, a subject and servant of the white British imperialists.

The waiter became increasingly irate when Ross told him that he should be speaking English instead of French. We could see that a fight might be in the offing and told Ross to stop. The waiter pointed out that he was not Indian but Vietnamese, and if Ross didn't want curried chicken, he had better leave. Ross had the curried chicken, ate the chicken but left the sauce. He queried the bill when the time came to pay because, since he hadn't eaten any of the sauce, he wasn't going to pay for it.

My brother told us later that the upstairs part of the building was the Paris headquarters of the Vietcong. Whether it was true or not, I do not know.

One morning, I was leaning against a pillar on one of the bridges over the Seine when I was suddenly pushed from behind in such a manner that I thought an apology was due. Confronting my assailant, I noticed he was holding a camera with extra lenses and all the paraphernalia that the press carry. Far from getting an apology, he shoved me again. The whole of the bridge was filling up with scuffling photographers, ducking this way and that, and in the middle of this mob were a couple of Brits, or should I say one and a half Brits, leisurely strolling.

It was probably the first and last time that the Duchess of Windsor had ever been asked to apologise for the behaviour of someone in her entourage, and her response was to raise her thin eyebrows and look the other way. I was then pushed back against the parapet until they had passed. I shouldn't think they wanted me in their pictures anyway.

To be clear, I am fairly certain it was the Duchess but have never been too sure, having always had a total disinterest in any of the toffs and normally wouldn't recognise one, even if they were to fall on my head.

The Berlitz Café was a hub and meeting place for musicians and artists, and at night, it got quite crowded. So when a couple of Algerians asked to sit with Ross and me at a street table outside the café, we said yes, and a lively conversation followed. The wine flowed, and in true North African style, our cigarette packets were placed on the table for anyone to help themselves. We each paid for our round of wine, but Ross became slightly alarmed when he realised he had to pay for his. He didn't mind taking everybody else's cigarettes while his stayed in his pocket, though.

Anyway, the night drew on, and our small gathering began to make music with glasses, bottles, my guitar, and the tabletop. It took on a distinctly North African tone, and the chugging rhythms only came to an end just before 3am Our poor waiter was dead on his feet and keen to shut the café. As we rose to leave, we noticed that we had gathered an audience from the large hotel across the road, the balconies crowded with onlookers.

One of the Algerians asked me to have dinner with him. His name, oddly enough, was Jimmy. He wanted to treat me to a typical Algerian meal, and we arranged to meet a couple of days later. I turned up for the appointment, but he didn't—likely a lack of pocket money, I assumed.

At night, walking back to Avenue de Messine, it was usual to pass the metro stations en route and glimpse, in the half light, a face rise above the steps, only to quickly duck back into the shadows. Elsewhere, one might see a couple of figures huddled together over the air vents to the underground. But the nights were hot, around twenty-three degrees, the pavements exuding heat, and the pissoirs in the street wreaking in the still air.

One early evening, my brother had arranged for us to meet up with his girlfriend, Irmela, her sister, and her sister's boyfriend, Jean, at the Berlitz Café, and then go on to Jean's place in the suburb of Choisy-le-Roi. We went by train, and reaching our destination, we started to walk to Jean's flat. For some reason, we attracted the attention of some North Africans who called out some abusive words. Jean shouted something back to them. Whatever it was that he said upset them very much, and they started to chase us along the street.

Irmela and her sister were wearing high heels, which were a bit of an impediment. Our assailants, however, were equally slowed down by being dressed in the usual striped Arab gowns and sandals. If it hadn't been so intimidating, it would have been funny. They had drawn their curved daggers, and clutching them above their heads with one hand whilst holding up the hems of their garments with the other, they clattered after us hooting and howling.

Turning a corner, we rushed into a bar and stayed there until the coast was clear. I still can't work out why the trouble started in the first place. I am sure that the aggressors wouldn't perpetually chase after people without good cause, and I wondered if there had been some earlier antagonism from Jean to bring this incident about—a case of cause and effect.

Some weeks later, when I had returned to England, my brother sent me a newspaper cutting reporting the machine gunning of that bar with several people killed and many more wounded. It was a very bad time for a many people, both Algerian and French.

I don't quite recall how I met Chris. He was not so much a beatnik but more a person imbibing beat culture. He had been in Paris for some time and had been fetching and carrying food for both Kerouac and Ginsberg. They had, he said, been hanging around in a warehouse that they had rented in Paris. When he said 'hanging around', it was less a metaphor than a reality. According to Chris, they had suspended themselves inside the building with ropes, and in a perpetual state of drug-induced euphoria, they refused to come down for days.

Chris kept me company for a good while, and in return, I paid for our lunches as he showed me around the shadier parts of town and the Latin Quarter. He took me to a café on Rue de la Huchette called Chez Popov, and to be truthful, despite my spending my time with a group of beats in London, I was way out of my depth in that place.

It was small, smoky, and very crowded with an assortment of beatniks, anarchists, communists, and little or no sign of the Pope to be seen. Everybody looked so worn out, with the smell of cannabis oozing from every skin pore. Some were lying on the pavement and others sitting, their backs against the walls of the adjoining buildings. At one point, a window on the top floor of a neighbouring house opened, and a woman poured the contents of a wash jug over those seated below. She neither warned us nor did her victims complain. They just rose and sat down elsewhere.

The whole episode seemed rather pointless.

There were too many young people with nothing to do except pass the day in exactly the same way as they had spent the day before. I suppose it was like working in a factory, repeating the same job over and over again, and losing the inclination to do anything else. Yes, it was great to be young in a new society, but I think it was too insular there, and they were losing sight of the outside world.

It's possible that a lot of those who spent time at Popov's made it into music or art later on in their lives. Others were obviously just passing through, but at that time, it was a bit too stifling, particularly in the heat of the day. We left after about an hour, and Chris and I moved off to an Algerian restaurant for couscous, salad, and a bottle of wine.

In those days, having such a scrawny neck, I had great difficulty finding a shirt to fit, so I took to wearing towelling tennis shirts done up at the neck with a silky, red, patterned cravat. It was not so much the scrawny neck or the towelling shirt that got them going but the cravat.

As I finished my meal with Chris and sat there with my stomach somewhat extended by the ingestion of couscous, they came across the floor, up my chair, and onto my lunch-swollen belly. There were five of them—tiny, full of fun, covered in fur, and determined to swing backwards and forwards on the end of my cravat.

Five lovely black and white kittens were making an assault on my clothing, three on my chest, one on my jacket sleeve, and one looking in my ear. With the rest of the wine to finish, that meal turned out to be one of the most enchanting lunches that I can recall.

When they finally got bored, off they went back into the kitchen. They were certainly a lot more entertaining than the crowd at Popov's.

The following day, we ate there again, but as we sat down, a friend of Chris' arrived.

'What are we having?' he asked.

I told him that we were all going to pay for our own food but could share a bottle of wine. He finished his meal in double-quick time, got up, and went to the counter in a pretence to pay. Instead, he told the cashier that I was paying, and off he went. In the end, I had to pay for his meal following threats that I couldn't understand. It was towards the end of my adventure in Paris, and I was already running out of cash, so it was really bad news.

Hardly a night went by without something happening which one might consider out of the ordinary. As I approached Place de l'Opera at about 2am, I could hear the roaring of car engines. There were three taxis racing at break-neck speed around the square, side by side, almost as if they were attached to each other. After the third circuit, a police van appeared, and the three split off instantaneously towards three different exits as if the escape had been well rehearsed. The police chased after none of them.

Carrying on along the boulevard, I heard a couple of gunshots, and passing the usual shadows of Algerians flitting back and forth in the half light, I eventually came within a short distance of Avenue de Messine. In the distance, the whine of a velo motor echoed through the silent streets, coming nearer every second.

Soon, it was too close to ignore, and I turned around to look. The bike had mounted the pavement and was heading straight at me. It was too dark to get a clear view of the rider, and taking no chances, I took my knife out just as the assailant was within a few yards of me. I swung around, knife in hand, to meet the attack.

The blade was only a couple of inches from his chest before I realised it was my brother. My knife skittered onto the paving stones under his wheels. He said that he thought it would be funny to scare me and watch me panic. It was quite frightening in all respects and not a bit amusing. Not only that, I had no idea that he had a motorised bike.

I was down to my last few francs, and it was time to leave. My friend Chris said that he would return with me, but he had been saying the same thing for weeks. To my surprise, he was at the station the next morning, ready to go. There were two or three others, including a girl from West Harrow about a mile from where I lived, and an aggravating and argumentative boy by the name of Mendleson or Mandelson, who had been accepted at university at the age of fifteen. It certainly didn't stop him from being an idiot, though.

Not much happened during the next few hours until we reached England and were about to board the London train when two customs agents decided to search our bags. None of us had anything illegal, but Chris' collection of books attracted their attention. Although they were French editions, they were all in English. Out of the fifty or so books, the agents felt sure that some of them were banned. In the meantime, the train was held up.

After a while, a list of banned editions arrived, and checking each one, they soon found that their suspicions were correct. They confiscated about a dozen or so books, including James Joyce's *Ulysses* and several publications mainly from one French publishing house (Obelisk, I think). The train eventually left the station about an hour and a half late.

When we arrived in London, I had seven shillings left and no francs. The girl from West Harrow was destitute and needed three shillings and nine pence to get home, and so did I. Chris left and went off to Wimbledon. I gave the girl half of my seven shillings, which I never saw again, not that I really expected to, and Mendelson I hoped to never see again and never did.

28

One evening, while sitting in a coffee bar in North Harrow and stretching the time it takes to drink a cup of coffee, an opportunity to make some money arose at last. It wouldn't pay much, just coppers, but it was better than nothing. The job entailed washing up the dishes and saucepans in the coffee bar.

I was quite used to washing up, having done much of it at home as a way of keeping out of my mother's firing line on her off days. I had learned that it was necessary to do a good job; otherwise, I would have to do it all over again. It was also a time of peace when I could reflect on the day and other things, the warm, stinking, greasy water acting as a balm to wash away the tribulations of never getting things quite right.

Washing up was good—good for my spirit, good for my soul, and something I could get right. The only problem was that I was only paid until midnight, but I was still washing up on most nights at 12.45am.

The wage was an astonishing two shillings and sixpence per hour, and if I could do two nights, it was worth one pound, five shillings to me. To make the gig a little more palatable, I was given a free plate of spaghetti Milanese and a cup of coffee each evening I worked there.

Chef Leo, a Polish man with a Scottish accent, was delighted with my work and praised me for my diligence. In fact, he was so impressed that he started to save all the saucepans that he had used during the week for me to clean. There were massive pans with Bolognese sauce caked around the inside up to an inch thick. The processed pea pans were in a similar state, and I can only say that it was with great relief that the chips fryer couldn't fit into the sink.

I queried as to why I should have all these extra pots to clean, and he would smile and say, 'You're the best washer-up that we've ever had. You are the only one who knows how to do it properly.'

He was seriously pleased and didn't understand that it was a little unfair that those who chose not to clean them got paid exactly the same as I did. The pans were never washed from the time I left the coffee bar on the Thursday night to when I returned the following Tuesday. I used to spend at least an hour cutting off the caked-on food with a sharp knife, soaking them for a while and then cutting some more away before they showed any glimpse of the metal.

Why did I do it? Why didn't I walk away? It's just the way I am. It didn't cost me anything, and I knew that if anybody died of food poisoning, it would have nothing to do with me.

The washing-up room was about five feet long and four feet deep, had two sinks side by side, and a gas water heater which leaked carbon monoxide into the tiny room. There was no ventilation, which made running the hot tap a life-threatening proposition.

To fill the sink, I would usually have to stand outside until the job was done, except when the bar was exceptionally busy. Then there was no escape. The dishes and cups would pour in, and I would just have to hold my breath for as long as possible until the water stopped.

The slops were emptied into two bins in the alley outside the kitchen door, and there, in quieter moments, I could go out to play with the rats. It has always amazed me that no matter how well one fixes the lid on top of a dustbin, the little dears always manage to get in.

I found that the best way to deal with them was to creep up to the bin, pull the lid off very sharply, and hold it in front of me. Those that jumped in my direction, instead of running up my front, hit the inside of the lid and fell back down into the bin, finally escaping on the second attempt and scurrying off down the alley in the opposite direction.

Those customers who indulged themselves with ham, either in a sandwich or a salad, would have been gratified to know that the hams were exceptionally well looked after. To keep them cool in summer and free from flies, they were hung from the metal rod that also supported the lavatory cistern and could then swing freely, directly over the WC.

The loo was in the alley, opposite the bins, and I always thought that standing to have a pee and having your nose pressed against a large lump of meat would be a little off-putting. But then again, there are those who might like to take advantage and have a crafty bite whilst relieving themselves.

The coffee bar manager had a problem with me, which was nothing unusual, and found it necessary to affirm his position as top dog by challenging me to a fight. I was surprised to have received such a generous offer and at first refused. This tended to make him a little more aggressive, and so, I eventually accepted his challenge.

One Thursday night, after the bar had closed at around 1am, we went out back for him to sort me out. He was a big chap, around six feet tall and quite a heavyweight, which made the whole thing appear even more bizarre. I could see that I had only two options: One was to win and therefore continue with his harassment, and the other was to lose and go home quicker. I chose the latter.

We moved round each other as if to grapple, and after a couple of lunges, I noticed that he was not the quickest fighter in the world. On his third attempt, I let him grab hold of me and pretended to struggle a little.

He put his arm round my neck and said, 'Give in now?'

'Yes,' I replied, and he let go.

He straightened himself out, bid me goodnight, and went back into the bar.

The following week, he was as friendly with me as if we were best mates and even increased my pay to fifteen shillings for an evening's work. I was in the big money now. Including my weekly allowance of ten shillings, I now had the grand sum of two whole pounds each week.

Working in the coffee bar had a couple of detrimental points. The first was that my clothes stunk of stale cooking, and the other was that eating the free spaghetti unsettled my system for a day or so. I always had cheese on it as opposed to the Bolognese sauce, trusting the latter even less than the cheese.

The bar was closed on the odd occasion by the Environmental Health for failing to carry out certain recommendations. These needed to be addressed if the bar were to remain open.

One of the demands was that the potato-peeling machine should be overhauled and cleaned out. The chef had dumped it outside in the alley hoping that the rain would do the job for him, but it didn't.

One evening on arriving for work, he presented me with a small knife and a half hundred-weight sack of potatoes. He said that there was no hurry as long as I had peeled them all by the time we got busy.

After half an hour, he came to collect those that I had finished. His face dropped. I am a potato carver, not a peeler. I will carve most of a potato away before I move on to the next.

He took the knife and the sack back into his kitchen, and taking a chair from the bar, proceeded to do the job himself. I was never asked again to peel the potatoes.

When I finally left, he telephoned me several times, begging me to return and even offered me more money. 'They don't know how to clean the pans. I have to do them myself.'

By that time, I had started working at Windsor and Newton's, and one hour of overtime there was worth more than five-hours' grind in front of a sink full of dirty, greasy plates.

29

One of the problems of living in a shoe box was that it was difficult to do anything that required concentration or solitude. I had taken to sitting up some nights in the living room, well into the early hours after my parents had gone to bed. It was my time to scribble down my own notion of poetry or verse or whatever one wishes to call it.

My girlfriend had introduced me to Keats, and by natural progression, I found Shelley, Bunyan, Blake, and Milton. Wordsworth's 'Daffodils' or Henry Reed's 'Naming of Parts' didn't do a lot for me, but the mysteries and fantasies of those that I called darker poets took a firmer grip on my mind.

I enveloped myself in a cloak which smothered all else in my brain for those few solitary hours as I dived into unearthly tunnels and met monsters face to face. At times, I felt I was outside my body. Ideas and scenes tumbled in, one after another, and jotting it all down turned much of it into an incomprehensible jumble.

My perpetual bouts of tonsillitis didn't help this near obsession either. When my coughing was at its worst, I could be found wandering about in the park in the middle of the night, taking in as much of the cold, clean night air as possible.

It was a magnificent time to be alone—to see a hedgehog amble across the field with its feet in the mist that lightly covered the ground, or an electric storm, silent but alight in a complete arc, with nonstop flickering branches of lightning all around. This is the magic of the night, the magic that fires the mind and fuels the imagination.

It was during this period that my brother had brought home a book with the intriguing title *The Vampire in Europe* by Montague Summers. I never saw him read it, but I certainly did. One of my favourite chapters was about the vampire of Croglin Grange, a story that I have since discovered appears to have its origins in the early seventeenth century.

There wasn't a proper door to our bedroom, but a curtain across the door space provided some privacy. There wasn't enough headroom to sit up straight, so to read this gripping tale, I had to sit scrunched forward with the book in front of me.

I had a reading light which was situated behind my head, so that most of the light was blacked out by my lack of transparency. The shadows that were cast about the little room were not ominous but gloomier in their aspect.

It was getting on for 2am.

My parents, in their rush to be modern, had taken to wearing rather unbecoming night clothes. My mother had started to parade about the house in a babydoll nightdress, and my father stumbled about in a pair of shorty, paisley-print pyjamas.

All was quiet in the flat. I had reached the section in the book where the vampire was picking the lead from around the small windowpanes with his long, horny fingernails. The curtain to my room suddenly swished back, and there stood a figure, his hairless, chicken-skin legs and knees glistening with a subdued greenish shimmer beneath his maroon paisley bulk and his underlit pastry-white face.

I jerked up in terror and caught my hair in the metal mesh of the upper bed frame, tearing out more than I felt was necessary before I came to realise that it was my father.

'What are you doing?' he inquired.

'Reading.'

'Oh!' he said, and with that, he pulled back the curtain and went back to bed.

It would have been better if he had stayed where he was instead of creeping around trying to spy on me. After that, I could never look at his shorty pyjamas ever again, whether stuffed with my father's rotundity or hanging on the washing line, without feeling the pain of losing all that hair.

As for my mother's costume—well, I couldn't imagine why she bought it or for what purpose, but the two of them could have been first-prize winners at any Halloween party for being the creepiest couple on the floor.

30

I was eighteen when my furry companion, Tibby, became ill. One of his kidneys was dead, possibly from being kicked by my mother, and the other was failing fast. Sadly, the vet had to end his existence. He was twelve years old.

In truth, he was the only one in the family that I had any feelings for, and he could always be relied upon to come to my rescue when things were bad. But life had to move on.

I couldn't really settle into any relationship for some time, having recently made a nuisance of myself with a Swedish girl that I'd met in Hastings—until I met Suzanne.

She was the third Jewish girl I had been out with. Being totally void of any religion myself, I have always failed to comprehend why it matters so much to parents to know that their daughter's boyfriend is in the same team.

Suzanne was lighthearted, petite, and liked to wear Mary Quant dresses---a 1960s girl ready to go. I don't think her parents were too enamoured of me when I met them the first and only time.

For some reason, some people believed that we were brother and sister and thought it was odd that we spent so much time out together. This became problematic when, while having lunch at an Italian dive on Wardour Street, the staff decided to test our family connection by demanding that we engage in some sort of incestuous act. It took us quite some time to understand if they were serious or just taking the piss out of us.

Three of the employees were standing around our table, coercing us to start kissing, and the chef, who was holding a meat cleaver, didn't look like he was going to give us any options.

Being the only ones left in the place, the situation seemed to be a little tricky, bearing in mind that we were in the basement. The only way out was up a narrow staircase.

We tried to cover our anxiety with humour, but the way they all kept looking at us was not very reassuring. Looking at the chef, one could easily imagine what would be his new entrée the following day, but what was more worrying was what might happen in between.

Still joking, we sidled off our bench seat and climbed the stairs to the main floor. It was necessary to pay the cashier at the till near the door. As luck would have it, he was unaware of what was going on downstairs.

One of the others was already halfway up the stairs, and I could see his friends were close behind him. We paid quickly and ran off down the street as fast as we could.

Suzanne was not allowed out most evenings, so on Fridays, I could always be found at Finch's with my old associates. Sue Miles was beginning to attract a significant amount of my attention, and not being able to sustain the thought of two relationships, I became a little confused.

What made matters worse was that Sue was a bit crazy in the nicest possible way. One night, she showed me her red can-can bloomers. That was even more confusing.

If I could have cloned myself, I could have led several independent lives, each with its own path, making it possible to see where each relationship was headed. But life's not like that.

This all came to a very odd turn of events. One night, Tibby appeared in a dream. He was much bigger, about my height, and walked on his hind legs. He approached me and we embraced. It was a strange pseudo-sexual embrace with his body pressed hard against mine.

Holding me firmly, he told me that I had to contact Cynthia as it could be my only choice in life. He was adamant about it. Then he calmly kissed me, turned, and faded away. That was my last encounter with my cat and confidant.

Taking his advice, I wrote to Cynthia the next day. A few days later, we met, and my other relationships ended. I had no doubt that my closeness to Tibby had conjured this epiphany. It was obvious that subconsciously, I still wanted to be with Cynthia despite a time lapse of well over a year. Nonetheless, it was a dream of such magnitude that I felt compelled to carry out his command.

I do wonder about what became of Suzanne and often think about her. As for Sue, I just hope that she's happy.

The previous year, I had asked my father to teach me to drive. After three lessons, the whole thing was stopped after leaving one man hanging onto the roof of a parked car, with my father in such fear that he could hardly utter a coherent word.

I received a small educational grant which my parents decided should be invested in a second-hand scooter, even though I really wanted a car. My brother had one, but his was new. The bike was a heavy 200cc Zundapp Bella which weighed about 3 cwt, but for all that, it was fast.

The first week, I crashed it into a parked car outside a garage. The car had just been resprayed and was out in the street waiting for its owner to collect it. I had been travelling slowly when the front wheel caught in a rut in the road. At the same time, a violent gust of wind blew into me from a side street, and their combined effort caused me to plough into the car.

Luckily, I was later tried and found fit to hold a driving licence. At least now, I had a means to travel at will. The scooter made my horizons just a little wider, and Cynthia and I could drive off to the Six Bells Jazz Club in Chelsea or Hastings whenever the mood hit us.

The Six Bells was an amazing club. It wasn't that large, being just the upstairs part of the pub, but the musicians who played there were some of the best in Britain, with Humphrey Lyttelton, Bruce Turner, Fat John, and Wally Fawkes all being regulars there.

The scooter was not a very safe way to travel, though. I was run off the road on one occasion by some cretins in a van who thought it was funny. Another time, I skidded on black ice for about forty yards without falling off, and after that, the bike slid on top of me in the snow when I tried to push it up a hill.

I only got hurt once but not seriously, which was quite fortunate. I had followed a drunken imbecile in a Rolls Royce up Blackbird Hill towards Neasden. His driving was so erratic that I tried to overtake him, but every time I tried, he swerved outwards, pushing me into oncoming traffic.

Finally, he abruptly stopped at a zebra crossing, and I moved up on the inside of his limousine. Once the crossing was clear, I moved off, but he had waved a van across in front of him, and I was hit on the side, the bike falling on my ankle.

It was not my fault, but the passenger of the van, a hostile old man with a nasty little face, jumped out and accused me of causing the accident, trying to gather support from the gathering crowd. I was still on the ground unable to get the bike off my leg.

The driver of the van came to my aid and told the old man to shut up and get back into his seat. He helped me up, and assessing the superficial damage, we decided that there was no serious harm done. It was only a short while later when I tried to brake that I found the drum on the front wheel had fallen apart.

On a rainy Saturday night, Cynthia and I returned to my flat as there was no point driving. Earlier, the roads had been flooded, and water had shot up the front of the scooter as I drove through the rivulets crossing my route on the way to collect her.

At eleven-thirty, the rain subsided, and we prepared to take Cynthia home. I put the key in the ignition, turned the lights on, and started the engine. There was a sizzling sound, then smoke started to pour out of the battery casing below the handlebars.

We retired to a safe distance and waited for the bike to blow up. After several minutes, the smoke died away; the lights were still on and the engine was still running. We got on and drove away.

I dropped Cynthia off at her house in Willesden Green and went home. When I finally got off the bike and turned the ignition off, the lights stayed on, and the engine continued to tick over. I put the key back in and tried again. Still the lights remained lit and the engine wound on. I turned the petrol supply off, but the lights stayed on, so I left it till the battery died.

In the morning, I looked inside the battery box and found that all the wiring for the entire system had welded itself into one massive wire, and there was no way to shut anything down. The repair was quite expensive. Obviously, driving in that kind of rain was not the thing to do.

During the Easter holiday of 1964, I set about looking for a job and, much to my amazement, found one packing artists' materials at Windsor & Newtons. The money was a far cry from Advance Laundry and made enjoying a good time much easier. In the summer, I returned and was paid even more money, around seventeen pounds a week. It didn't matter that I had failed all my A levels. I now had a job and loved every moment.

31

It's difficult to say when my bad habit started. Was it the first sip of South African Burgundy from a screw cap flask, my grandfather's potato wine, or the Beaujolais at my first all-night party. But whatever the incentive, wine gradually became a significant interest for me. By 1960, I had become quite immersed in its delights. Needless to say, my palate was still untrained and often sullied by tobacco and bad air.

In 1964, with some strong-arm coercion from my family, I ended up leaving the packing job I loved for work in the wine trade, which put me on a path that has plagued me ever since.

Coercion might be a strange word to use for entering a profession in which I could indulge myself in one of the great pleasures of life, but truth to tell, it was not my choice. I had been earning a good wage at Windsor & Newtons, had no travelling expenses or other costs, and was able to give Cynthia four pounds a week to save for me.

At twenty, I still had no clue as to my future plans, and my extended education seemed all rather pointless. I was qualified to work in an office, but what I really liked best was manual work and would have been happier to be a road sweeper than a clerk in an office. The problem was my parents and their incessant cribbing about me working in a factory. While I was doing my best to figure out my future, I had to endure relentless nagging from them.

'I'm not having a son of mine working in a factory!'

'After all we've done to give you a good education!'

The call was also taken up by my brother, who regularly gave my mother advice on what future career I should follow. I finally caved in to the perpetual torrent of unsolicited advice and applied to several London wine merchants for employment.

I was offered a job by one company, and I should have known that it would not be in my best interest to take it when a disturbing event occurred just before my interview.

It happened in Crutched Friars, a street behind Fenchurch Street station, as I approached the offices of Brooks, Bodle & Co. Across the road, I saw two men fiddling around under a parked lorry. A third man in his sixties was walking along the pavement towards them, and as he drew level, the two under the lorry sprang out and beat him to the ground with baseball bats. Grabbing his briefcase, they made off through a passage that led to the station.

I ran across the road to the man who was lying on his back on the pavement, bleeding from several gashes on his head, his smashed glasses askew across his face. I tried to comfort him while looking out for some assistance.

The man was terrified and begged me not to hit him again. I supposed I had arrived so quickly that he must have thought I was one of his attackers. A crowd had quickly gathered, and I asked them to call for the police and an ambulance. And then I slipped into Brooks Bodle for my interview.

When I came out into the street after the interview, there were several policemen and detectives standing around the injured man, and as I appeared, it seemed that I had attracted their attention as well. Indeed, I became the chief suspect, and it was only my concern for the old man that got them to listen to what I had to say.

Apparently, the old chap only remembered me and was convinced that I was one of those who had hit him. I was glad that his injuries had not damaged his brain because the description he gave them was quite accurate.

I spent the next couple of hours at Fenchurch Street police station studying hundreds of photos of violent criminals. I could see none that I recognised in the books, but on the wall in front of me was the face of someone wanted for murder. The image staring out from the poster looked familiar and was one I did not wish to see again.

I thought for a while and decided against mentioning it. If the man were caught, the murder charge would be enough to ensure his detention, but the idea of testifying against him in court on another charge would probably not be a very safe thing to do, especially since there was some doubt in my mind as to his being one of the robbers.

Mr Ling, the main director of Brooks Bodle, offered me a position as the understudy to the company secretary at the pathetic wage of nine pounds, ten shillings a week, with luncheon vouchers included. It was necessary for me to shave off my little wispy beard and get a shorter haircut.

My mother was delighted for all of five minutes until she found something else to have a go at, like the woman next door, and remained deaf to my declaration that I would have no money left over for myself at the end of the work week.

With the vague hope that the job might lead to a career, I accepted the offer. My mother, thinking that I was now in the big time—'My son works in the city, you know'—demanded another pound for my keep, leaving me next to broke.

What really aggravated me was when I saw her on one occasion handing the money that I had just given her to my brother, who was unemployed at the time. He had been sacked from his job in a wine shop in Pinner for theft of bottles from the owner's private cellar. So now he got his dole money and my keep money so he could go out and have a good time while I was left stoney.

Working at Brooks Bodle did have some benefits. There was wine to be tasted, at times wine to be drunk, and on the odd occasion, the chance to get drunk. The beauty of the latter is hard to define: some drink out of despair, others out of carelessness, indifferent to what they consume.

Then there are those chasing an instant buzz—drinking meths or surgical spirit if they are poor, or Bacardi, vodka, pastis, gin, or whisky if they have money or wealthier friends.

There are still others who don't intend to have one for the road but do, and those who cannot bear to see a delectable libation poured down the plughole. I have a tendency to fit into the last category.

Each time I consider getting rid of something, I try to evaluate its creation. Polythene bags I find easy to put in the rubbish, but to pour a full seventy-five centilitres of Chateau Petrus 1953 down the sink takes a lot of consideration, and I had only twenty minutes in which to consume it.

It really wasn't right, especially when I got drunk. In my debatable defence, I hasten to add that after a good meal, I am loathe to chuck away the remains of a cheese and garlic sauce and will secretively stick a spoon in the saucepan to retrieve the last vestige before I immerse it in the washing-up bowl. To explain more fully the context of this Château Petrus, it was my job and a favour to Mr Ling to clear up the tasting room.

Each month, the directors of Brooks Bodle and the parent company, Williams & Humbert, would hold a board meeting and luncheon, and it was for Brooks Bodle to supply the wine from its cellars.

If Jean Calvet—whose agency we held—arrived, then the wine had to be superlative, usually Petrus.

Mr Ling would always decant the bottles and only to the last third of the bottle. Hence, three bottles of decanted Petrus equalled three-thirds left in the bottom of the bottles, which made for a full bottle with nearly no sediment.

The present value of this amazing wine is around €3600 per bottle, which is a great shame because at that price, few of us ever get the chance to taste it. Most of the people who have the wine in their cellars don't drink it either. So what is the point of making it in the first place?

To describe the event more fully, it is necessary to start at the foot of the stairs to the tasting room. As I opened the lower door, the bouquet was so powerful that it cascaded down the stairs and nearly took my breath away. It was the most exquisite wine aroma I had ever known.

By the time I reached the room, I had no idea that this was the highly rated Chateau Petrus I was smelling. I had a taste of most of the other top wines over the preceding weeks, and though impressed, nothing could match the sheer beauty of this wine.

My only regret was that I drank the lot instead of pouring it into one bottle and taking it home for Cynthia and me to enjoy. I think it was Petrus that the gods on Olympus drank and not some sloppy elixir, and it was that which may have accounted for some of their shenanigans.

I had not worked in an office before and found that, though the work was boring, the colourful personalities who carried out the work were all quite interesting. Mr Ling was the engine of the company. He liked classical music and suffered from stomach ulcers, which at times made him quite irascible. He liked me and treated me very politely with plenty of encouragement. He did get angry with me on one occasion but apologised soon after.

Arthur Presman was the company secretary and Mr Ling's right-hand man. He was a rather nervy character who found it difficult to relax in the office and seemed to be fearful of his boss.

Mr Bach was the company accountant, and having his desk at the far end of the office, it was necessary for Mr Ling to bellow 'BACH!' every time he wanted to speak to him. Mr Bach was a little overweight, terrified of Mr Ling, and only managed to keep his weight under control by running subserviently up and down the office hall every time he got 'the call'. He also liked walking in the country and sleeping under his newspaper at almost any time of the day. When he was awake, he could be quite animated and interesting but his excessive grovelling was upsetting to witness.

Mr Mellor was the 'post boy' and didn't like me very much. I believe that this was due to his thinking that I was there to replace him, which was about as far off from my intentions as one could imagine. He did, however, spend some time trying to teach me the intricacies of the postal franking machine, whose mysteries flew way above my head, irritating him even more. Poor chap, to be almost seventy years old and have to put up with such obstinacy!

When I arrived, there were two typists and an office junior. When I left, there were none; all had been enticed by better wages elsewhere. What was odd was that in the absence of qualified typists, it became necessary to employ agency staff at a greater cost.

As the company gradually lost its identity, being overwhelmed by the parent company, Williams & Humbert, I had to learn to type, albeit with one finger, but it was the only way left to sort out the insurance for shipping the wine.

One morning, the typing agency sent a young woman to the office who was, to all intents and purposes, a good worker. She settled down quickly and quietly to work, but I felt sure that there was a problem building in the office.

She was Black, and I heard somebody say, 'What would they think if they came into the office and saw a Black woman working here?'

I'm unsure from whence the directive came, but she was returned to the agency and soon replaced by a less efficient, younger white woman whose language was more coloured than her predecessor's skin. She didn't last long either.

The advertising manager for Williams & Humbert had an office on the same floor as Brooks Bodle, and seeing him swanning past on a few occasions, I was not so impressed by his impresario persona but more by his beard.

Noting that there were others with beards in the building, I took it as carte blanche to grow mine once more. It had hardly got underway when I was asked once more to shave it off, this time as a directive from the advertising department on the pretext that only top people were allowed to have facial hair.

I didn't mind too much; it never grew that well anyway, and it gave me the excuse to snigger quietly when walking past him.

The first time I met with dishonesty in the trade, it surprised me. An order had arrived for a sample of Pommard 1961 wine, London bottled. Normally, all Brooks Bodle stocks were bottled in the customs-bonded warehouse of Thomas Trapp, but at the time, the company was waiting for a new shipment of Pommard and only had Volnay available as the closest comparable wine.

The customer did not want Volnay—it had to be Pommard. In desperation and not wishing to lose the order, Mr Ling dispatched me to Trapp's warehouse to collect one bottle of Volnay. Back in the office, a Calvet Pommard label was affixed, and it was sent off to the customer.

Mr Ling was not happy but said we could not afford to lose an order or the customer. This was the only occasion when I saw this done, and I suppose, bearing in mind that the wine was the same price, the deception was not as serious as it could have been.

As the year progressed, I had started commuting to work on my scooter, with the added benefit of whizzing around London delivering samples to various clients during the day. It was on such an errand that I ended up at the Old Vic with samples of wine and fine cognac to hand to the catering manager.

The request for the samples had come through Blundell, the representative for Williams and Humbert, a young chap in his twenties who was having certain problems getting orders.

The catering manager asked me directly, 'What do you really think of these samples that you have brought?'

I was happy to assure him that they were excellent products from one of the most prestigious wine shippers in France and could guarantee the quality. He explained that the samples were to be tasted by a panel which included Lawrence Olivier, and he expressed some puzzlement that Blundell seemed less knowledgeable than the delivery boy.

I thought no more about it until a few weeks later when Blundell approached me in the cellars and thanked me for helping him out. He had received a huge order from The Vic, which the manager had told him was mainly down to me. I didn't get anything from it financially, but it was good news and quite gratifying.

Blundell lost his job a few months later but still kept the company car, an Austin Maxi, as part of a payoff.

Not only was it cheaper going to work on my bike rather than using the train, but I could experience a little amusement along the way. One time, as I approached the end of the Edgware Road to cut through the back of Oxford Street, I became entrenched in a swiftly moving diplomatic motorcade, complete with police motorcycle outriders. I had somehow tagged onto one of the African heads of state, though I don't know which one, but I quickly picked up the end of it.

As each set of traffic lights was approached, whether red or green, one of the police motorcyclists would block the traffic from the side streets. Nobody seemed to worry about me following the procession, and the policemen just waved me through each time.

The special treatment was strange since my face was obscured completely by my scarf and old flying goggles. Maybe it was my funny old French police motorcycle helmet that did the trick. The outcome was that I arrived at work forty minutes early, which shocked everybody.

Calvet fine wine distributors were in the process of promoting their range of top-quality cognac, and it was decided to give the product a showing at the Royal Garden Hotel in Kensington. I had to be there by eight in the morning to help set up the tables and display the cognac, glasses, and wine. It was quite an important event and was led by Brooks Bodle's managing director, Mr P.

It was a very stuffy affair with lots of old-school ties and people who preferred to burn their palates with strong liquor than to savour the eloquence of a large glass of good wine. I admit that the cognac was not for the fainthearted. With prices exceeding several weeks' wages for a Baccarat decanter filled with Grande Champagne Cognac, it was obviously a show designed for the wealthy and not for the likes of me.

The promotion was a morning event. Mr P ordered me to guard the remaining stocks while he and his friends went off to lunch just in case any of the hotel staff were tempted to help themselves. He said that somebody would bring down a salad for me, and off he went.

I had gotten up at six fifteen that morning, and by half past two, no food had arrived. One of the staff told me to go to the kitchen, but they too were closed. Finally, everything had been cleared away—the tables gone, the cognac packed away—and by a quarter to five, I decided to leave, still having had nothing to eat since breakfast. Obviously, Mr P had failed to mention that I needed to be fed, and I was not very happy, to say the least.

This incident had not gone unnoticed by another member of the party. A couple of days later, as I took the lift to the office, Mr Alexander, son of the chairman of Williams & Humbert, thanked me for my contribution to the event and slipped a five-pound note into my pocket. It was greatly appreciated and went a long way to soothe my aggravation. I know it was only a fiver, but it was still half my week's wage.

Despite the interest Mr Ling had shown in pushing me forward, it was obvious that without the right education or the right tie, there was absolutely no chance of moving up in the London wine trade, particularly with Mr P as managing director. He appeared to have taken an instant dislike to me and seemed solidly determined to keep me in my place.

Though he was Chairman of the Wine Trade Association, it did not preclude him from ignoring my application form to take the course set up by the Association to promote workers within the trade. Basically, it meant that if I passed the initial examination, my wage would be significantly increased to a figure set out by the Association.

The Wine Trade Association was also responsible for training students to achieve the grade of Master of Wine, which could have been fun. Having handed him my application personally, I was a little disappointed that I never received the necessary course details, and on telephoning his office at the Association, his secretary informed me that there was no trace of my application to be found. Assuming that he had destroyed it, I gave notice to quit a few days later.

32

Having left Brooks Bodle, I now had to come up with plan B. It was obvious that I had to leave home. There was absolutely no reason to stay any longer. In fact, I should have left when I was two. I announced the plan to my mother first and later to my father when he returned that evening.

He was devastated. He stood in the doorway of my bedroom in his horrid shorty pyjamas, his chicken-skin legs glinting in the half-light and sobbed, 'Who's going to look after us in our old age?'

He was forty-seven years old. If I could have left at that instant, I would have done. So that was what he had in mind for my future.

Besides everything else, my brother had the infuriating habit of taking my scooter on weekends if I had my back turned, despite having his own bike, and would leave me without transport for several days. He would then return it with an empty tank, without so much as a thank you.

I needed to distance myself from my toxic home environment before it was too late. The insidious seed of guilt had been deeply planted in my psyche, lying dormant until my mother chose to awaken it, which she did with alarming frequency. I had had enough—I was a capable adult now, and I had Cynthia.

As Cynthia had said time and time again, "If only you had stayed at Windsor & Newton's, found a flat, and got out of their lives without leaving a forwarding address, it would all have been different.' And she was right.

Cynthia and I packed a few possessions onto the back of the scooter and left for Hastings. The new adventure had begun. And to start it off with a bang, as we approached Robertsbridge on the A21 just after dark, the rear tyre blew.

The bike, now relying on one wheel and travelling down a long winding hill, became impossible to control. It bucked like a mule from side to side and up and down. Within a few seconds, Cynthia took off over my head and crashed into the road a little ahead of the bike. I soon followed and remember seeing her sliding in front of me on her side, one arm forward and her left leg raised.

Looking behind for a moment, I could see the bike still upright and gaining on us, apparently determined not to miss out on the fun. Eventually, it too fell over and skidded after us.

Looking in the opposite direction, I could see the traffic coming up, round the bend, their headlights heading straight towards us as we continued to slide towards the middle of the road. We both thought, time's up, but we obviously weren't quite ready.

The traffic stopped and people rushed over to see if we were all right and, amazingly, we both were. Someone pulled their car up onto the grass verge so that I could change the wheel in their headlights, and about an hour later, we were back on the road. The only damage was to our boots and the fairings of the scooter.

We stayed for a while with a friend and found some temporary work picking hops at the Guinness Farm in Bodiam. Sunny days, fresh beer, and cheese sandwiches were all that one could wish for, with the bright eyes of youth glistening in the sunshine.

After that came apple picking at Icklesham and with it, the October mists that blotted out the early morning to leave a heavy dew on the grass. The work was not as good with lower pay than at the hop farm. We were paid one shilling and a penny for picking a bushel of apples.

On inspection, if a single bruise or fingernail mark was found on any of the apples in the box, the pay dropped to a single penny. We were selected to fill massive crates with tiny apples under the same conditions, and our wages dropped even more. But the days were warm, and our adventure continued.

We moved with our host to a little house in Hastings, and trying to economise, we attempted to live on what I thought was a pot au feu without the meat. We kept it going for a couple of weeks but began to feel ill; I think it had gone a bit septic. Soon, it was time to take life a little more seriously and find more permanent work.

The days of youthful dreams were quickly drawing to a close.

33

One of the best things about living by the sea was finding the most unexpected things along the beach, particularly early in the morning. Cynthia had to leave for work long before I did, and in the intervening hour, I would often pass the summer mornings strolling along the shingle.

Finding a dead dog washed up on the beach was a sad thing and made me wonder how the poor creature ended its days in the sea. Another oddity was the bare skull of a medium-sized cod with a large tapeworm inside its cavity. It was hard to fathom how such parasites could live in salt water apparently unaffected and how they ended up inside the fish's head.

I found a long piece of beechwood which, once dry, I shaped into the neck of my homemade twelve-string guitar. There was plenty of this sort of stuff lying about, a kind of life after death in the detritus of the waves.

Lumps of tar were constantly appearing along the tideline, and as the 1960s progressed, the amount of tar increased and, insidiously, so did the number of dead seabirds. They were often almost unrecognisable by the amount of tar that enshrouded them. It was a constant tragedy and still is with hardly any responsibility ever taken by those who pollute the sea, whether with oil, plastics, or chemicals.

Even seabed dredging is licensed and encouraged by our government. The effects are horrendous and often negate all the things that some do to help other creatures get by.

It was on one of those sunny summer mornings before the holiday makers crowded the beach that I saw the tiny figure sitting not far from the water's edge. I soon realised that it was a guillemot that had been washed up and was just sitting there exhausted, unable to fly. It had just one small spot of oil on its breast.

I sat down a few yards from it and spoke to it softly, which seemed to soothe it. I stayed with the bird for some time until it appeared completely relaxed and allowed me to pick it up, place it in a cardboard box that I had found, and take it back home.

While I had breakfast, it sat on the table and looked around as I stroked it, which it seemed to like. Eventually, off we went to work. It sat in the shop without any apparent fear while we waited for the man from the RSPCA.

He was very business-like. Taking a wicker cage from his van along with a pair of thick leather gauntlets, he said, 'Get a lot of these, we do. Guillemots, diving birds, you know.'

Thrusting his large, gloved hand into the box, he grabbed my new friend around the neck and thrust it into the basket. The bird was terrified and fought viciously against the rough hand with its long sharp bill. Had I known that this was the way he dealt with these poor creatures, I would have taken the bird back home, but I had no idea how to look after it or clean it and was sure the professionals would do a better job than I. Had he asked, I would have put the bird in the basket myself without any fuss.

I inquired what the next step would be as he walked away, and nonchalantly, he replied, 'Oh, we'll probably put this one down. It's too far gone.'

By the way the bird had attacked him, I thought that it had plenty of life left in it and was horrified by his response. I just hoped that he was wrong and that the people who look after these precious creatures were more optimistic than he was.

I tend to believe that we are no better as a species than any other life forms, and I don't think that we have more right to exist than other creatures. This probably does not go down well with a lot of people, but many of us have pets and treat them as individuals with their own personalities. This in itself shows respect for them, and they in turn often give us love and loyalty in their own ways. Like us, they just want to live.

The more one involves oneself with nature, the more beautiful it becomes, and though it takes time that could be spent on other things, it has made me realise that I am just part of the fabric of the world, just a short length of hay in a vast haystack and, really, just another animal.

To see the way that one small creature in the wild defends its young against a more insidious animal is totally amazing. I can still see in my mind the tiny undersized rabbit we called Hunk. She had two babies in our garden under a paving stone that leaned up against the greenhouse.

We called them Roly and Carter. When her babies were quite tiny, we saw Hunk chasing off two large rats that were threatening to steal them from her, and she really meant business.

We had found her in the garden, not much bigger than a mouse when she decided to adopt us. She liked to have toast for breakfast and could be seen running down from the woodland every morning to greet us. I would comb out her fleas as she lay on the grass in the sunshine, and she repaid us by leaving her babies in the vegetable plot.

It was a short, memorable affair. Myxomatosis took both her and her boyfriend, 'the Bean', and the traffic killed her children, both of whom used to snooze under the plum tree outside the kitchen door.

There was also the rare family of striped field mice which suddenly took up residence in our attic. To see them play hide-and-seek in the rockery and chasing each other around like children at a birthday party was an absolute delight.

Unfortunately, our neighbour was less enthralled and poisoned them. The toxin made them seek out water, and several of them entered our cold-water tank and died. We used the same water to wash in and clean our teeth, and it was only when pieces of decomposed flesh and fur started to appear in the bathroom sink that we found out what had happened to our little guests.

I think it's time we all woke up, not just some. Poison is not the answer. There is always a chain reaction, whether in the countryside or in the town, and you may one day find your precious cat or dog dead from catching a dying mouse.

We had some house mice in Hastings at one time who became a bit of a nuisance, so we bought a humane trap. There were forty-four of them, and they all agreed as we released them under the hedge that the cheese was very nice.

34

Cynthia had a little money for us to live on for a few weeks until I eventually found employment in probably the lowest paid place outside the City of London. I was back in the wine trade at Foster's Wine Merchants.

It was all right for a short period of time as a stop gap, but anybody with any interest in wine would drown in the abysmal flow of old folks bringing back their Guinness bottles for replacement.

Then there were those who were hooked on sweet red or white fortified wine made from the waste product of legitimate wine fermentation. In other words, it was made from the stuff left over in the bottom of the cask after the wine was run off. This residue had sugar, water and yeast added and would then be re-fermented.

At the end of its fermentation, alcohol was added to produce a drink that had tramps lying in gutters and old people out of their shells in geriatric homes all over the country—that is, if they didn't die before they got there.

People worried about cannabis, but this was far more dangerous and benefited from a lower duty than other more legitimate products, such as port or sherry. Foster's had its own wine brand which sold for a little over seven shillings a quart. One could see the impact over a short period on people who bought the stuff and didn't last more than a few months.

It was not unusual for a new customer to buy a bottle, which could last them a week. After a couple of months, they would be drinking up to three quarts of wine a week, and then suddenly, they'd disappear. They were usually single female pensioners, the old men having already passed on.

The wine was sold as British Sherry or British White or Ruby Port and had as much to do with sherry or port as a bowl of porridge. The high sugar content tended to dispel hunger, and the high alcohol content numbed the mind, eventually destroying it.

It was nothing unusual for a customer to start asking for credit when their pension could no longer take the strain. This was always the marker for losing a customer. Fortunately, the stuff is no longer available (I hope) unless one is unlucky enough to find a cache under a dead relative's bed.

The manager at Foster's was a bit of an oddity. He had a good side to his nature and also a crappy, stupid side which could make him totally unbearable. He had been trained at a Peter Dominic shop and had a good general knowledge of wine. What he didn't like was that I seemed to know more than he did about clarets and Burgundies.

To trip me up, one Saturday morning, he offered me a glass of claret. 'If you're so clever, smarty pants, tell me what this is.'

The test was pathetic. We had in stock only half a dozen good quality wines, and I had noticed that one had disappeared from the shelf since the previous day. We didn't sell that class of wine that often. The missing bottle was Chateau Lagrange 1957, and just outside the office, I had seen the empty bottle in the waste-glass bin.

I smelled the wine. It was positively a St. Julien with a bit of age, and the rest was simple. I swilled it around in the glass, sniffed it again, tasted it drawing air through my lips, hummed a little and said, 'I might be wrong, but I would say this is a 1957 St. Julien, and by the style and composition, I would go for Chateau Lagrange, 3rd growth from the 1855 classification of Bordeaux Red Wines.'

He stood there with his mouth wide open, incapable of speech. I couldn't leave it there, so I admitted the truth to try to make him feel better, but it seemed to make matters worse because I had made a fool of him. Sometimes one just can't get it right.

His children raided the crisp rack every day saying that they *needed* some crisps or *needed* some other junk food, which was very irritating. It rather undermined the meaning of children in need.

I also found the constant question, 'What are you?' very aggravating and idiotic, which did nothing to encourage me to respect him.

I think the worst bit was when I announced that I was going to get married and needed to have the day off. He refused and threatened to sack me. It was only through his wife trying to talk sense into him that he finally agreed.

He was keen to build up the business, particularly through the wholesale side, and to do this, he and his wife would visit the local restaurants to encourage the proprietors to open accounts with the shop. It was an expensive effort, and his wages were definitely not able to cover the costs. Therefore, he tried to do it through the petty cash.

There is a limit to how far one can go down this route, but he seemed unaware of it. A little after I had left to go to Ellis, Son & Vidler, he was taken to court by the parent company and was found guilty of theft.

One day, the police arrived at the shop to tell me to move my brother's car from a triangle of gardens in the centre of Lamberhurst on the A21. My brother had left his car with a young policeman from Hastings, who apparently had been in the process of buying it. In the meantime, my brother had gone off to Australia as a steward on the SS *Oriana*.

He had left the registration documents with me to hand over to the buyer once the money had been paid in full. I refused to have anything to do with the car since it was not my responsibility, and I would only end up paying for its removal.

I later became aware of the events that led up to the vehicle being dumped. It was crashed just outside Lamberhurst on the way to London by the policeman who bought it. In the back was a registered heroin addict who was involved with a London crime syndicate and was occasionally called upon to scare or eliminate certain individuals. He had been given a gun by one of the syndicate's contacts in Hastings's Old Town.

To keep him calm and under control, she had also given him an extra dose of heroin for the trip. The target was apparently 'hit' by somebody else a few days later since the car never arrived at its destination.

It was fortunate for my brother that he was away for a whole year; otherwise, he might have become personally involved in the situation. Both the policeman and the woman from the old town were later arrested and jailed for drug-related crimes. And that was the end of another 2.5 litre 1947 Riley RMB.

I was not a stranger to weird natural phenomena, but this one took the biscuit. Speaking to an ex-policeman one day about the odd things that he had seen in the past, he related that while on duty one night on Robertson Street in Hastingst, he heard a shushing sound. The noise grew in intensity as he stood there in a shop doorway.

At first, he could see nothing, but then became aware that the road appeared to be moving. He soon realised that he was seeing the mass exodus of cockroaches from the town centre, and the noise was from thousands of cockroach feet. The massive column turned left at the old Henneky's Wine Bar building and disappeared.

While chatting a while later with a female customer about one of the restaurants nearby, she declared, 'Oh, I used to have a flat above that one, but I left after a frightening experience one night.

'I was living on the second floor when I heard a tapping and scratching at my window in the middle of the night. I thought it might have been a bird trying to get in, so going over to the bedroom window, I looked out, or rather, tried to. The glass was covered by thousands of cockroaches which were clambering up the outside wall searching for a way in.'

I had scarcely believed the policeman's tale, but her story corroborated it, and I admit that I would've loved to have seen it.

After I left Foster's, I joined an old Hastings wine merchant, Ellis, Son & Vidler. They had just acquired the seafront premises of another local off-licence, Glenister's, and were looking for a manager to run the shop.

The main reason they had bought the place was for the extensive handmade caves which penetrated the sandstone cliff by up to one-hundred and twenty feet. These had been used by smugglers in earlier times and were once part of the no-go area of Old Time Hastings.

Originally, the caves would have been much longer, but the cliff had been blasted away to make a new road along the seafront during the early nineteenth century. Walking along the waterfront at White Rock, one couldn't tell that almost every shop had one or more of these massive caves running into the rock behind it.

The local director of Ellis, Son & Vidler was Freddie Snow, who had started as a delivery boy in the early 1920s. He was sufficiently impressed with my enthusiasm for wine and, having received a glowing report from Mr Ling at Brooks Bodle, he took me on as a manager-in-training for their soon-to-be-opened White Rock Shop.

While the new shop was being sorted out, I was installed at Adelaide House, the impressive late Georgian residence of Queen Adelaide, the wife of William IV. The ground-floor shop was unchanged from Victorian times with wood panelling and a tall mahogany counter which towered above the customers.

Mr Freddie Snow was really the mastermind behind the company's local success. He was a mason and friends with all the Tory elite, most of whom actually ran the town. He was famous for the amount of Amontillado Crown Sherry he consumed during the course of one day. Usually affable, particularly when slightly mellow, he could often be heard singing to himself as he wandered off to his car.

On one occasion, he left the cellars in such a state of ine-briation that whilst trying to unlock his car, he fell back-wards into the road. Two local traffic wardens who knew him well, picked him up and gently eased him into the dri-ving seat.

It was nothing unusual for him to be in that state or near it, but it was unlikely that he would ever be stopped unless he ran somebody over.

Mr Snow had at one time decided that when he retired, I would take over from him. He started to explain how he used the petty cash to double his income every week. On most mornings, he would call me into his office to start the day's consumption, and when I returned to my work after one glass, it was not unusual to see through the rippled glass his elbow lift several more times.

Occasionally, he would top up my glass for a second round, and loose-tongued, he would divulge personal stories that would have been better left unsaid.

During the war, he had been enlisted as a private, and because of his age and experience in the wine trade, he was sent off to Europe with the Navy, Army, and Air Force Institutes. He eventually served in Italy and soon became involved in the black marketing and exchange of NAAFI property. He ended up with quite a lucrative business selling to the officers champagne, caviar, and any other luxuries that he'd been able to trade with the locals in exchange for some of the NAAFI commodities.

He remembered delivering wine and groceries as a boy to Rider Haggard in St. Leonards in the early 1920s. The list of now long-forgotten local celebrities who had come to the shop was impressive, and it was easy to see that he had imbibed not a small dose of self-importance from their association.

It was standard practice to import wine in casks and bottle it in England. With honest merchants, the contents of a bottle were as labelled. However, greed and in some cases criminality in certain unscrupulous enterprises would overpower the otherwise old order of the wine trade. Ellis, Son & Vidler began to suffer under the new regime.

It surprised me to find that three wines were being sold under a multitude of different labels. Red Burgundy 4103,

Red Bordeaux 984, and the unnumbered White Burgundy were all sold under no less than a dozen generic titles. I didn't know when the practice had started, but it seemed to be accepted as a legitimate part of the business.

Unfortunately, once one is set on such a path, it inevitably leads to an extension of the abuse, which I found extremely difficult to condone. It was all very well to say that the customers didn't know any better, but they were indeed being duped and paid good money for that privilege. The practice was not confined to Ellis, Son & Vidler but to a great many of the more commercial vintners throughout Britain.

One of the most bizarre additives used to 'body-up' some of the thinner wines was the addition of baby milk powder. It brings to mind the extraordinary destruction of two casks of a fine Tavel Rosé shipped by one of Burgundy's most revered négociants, Louis Jadot. On arrival, it was deemed that after bottling, it would be too expensive to sell quickly and therefore needed to be cut with a similar quantity of the cheap white Burgundy.

Louis Jadot labels were reproduced at a local printers, and the wine was put up for sale. It sold quite well but was soon being returned on account of its fizziness—it had started to re-ferment. The whole of the remaining stock along with the returns were put back into casks, dosed with sulphur dioxide to stop the fermentation, bulked out with milk powder, forcibly pumped through a massive filter, and re-bottled as Chinon Rosé. It successfully sold out on a special offer list.

The vineyards of Chinon and Tavel were a long distance apart, and to kill a fine wine to produce a fake chemical hotch-potch was, to my mind, greed gone mad.

One morning, one of the regular old ladies who used to shop at Foster's appeared in the doorway of the White Rock Shop. Armed with two bags of empty Guinness bottles, she trundled her way into the shop like one of Andy Capp's characters, passed the rows of carefully laid out wines, and plonked one bag on the counter and the other on the floor.

'You're here now, are you? she said as she unzipped the bag on the counter. I leaned forward to see what she was about to produce when suddenly, a huge spider leaped out from between the bottles and landed squarely in the middle of my chest. I felt its heavy bulk as it hit me, and I was absolutely certain that I heard it make a shrill scream as it landed on my shirt. I scudded backwards in absolute terror towards the cellar. It fell off and scurried away under the counter.

In the meantime, the old lady seemed totally unaware of what had happened, and pulling out one of the empties, she asked for three refills and a quart of British Ruby Wine, none of which we stocked. It took me ten minutes to convince her that it was not the same kind of shop as Foster's, and all the time, I kept glancing round in case the face hugger was creeping up on me. I never saw it or the lady again.

As a child, I had developed an enthusiasm for certain comedians, the ones who did not appear to be too impressed by their own performances. My favourite was Tommy Cooper. He was very tall, always wore a fez onstage, and had a charming, surprised, self-effacing laugh when one of his magic tricks turned out right. So when he walked into my shop and asked for a bottle of champagne, I was totally delighted.

I told him that I had always admired his work and hoped that his performance at the White Rock Theatre had gone well and chatted with him for a little while. He paid for the champagne and asked for a receipt.

I asked, 'In whose name shall I make it out?'

He replied, 'Put it down to me'—and that's where it all went wrong.

I couldn't for the life of me remember his name! Embarrassed, I timidly said, 'I don't wish to be offensive, but I have a slight problem. I can't remember your name'.

Having told him that he'd been a favourite of mine since childhood, how could I not remember his name? It was unforgivable. He gave me one of those looks as if I was making fun of him, and realising that I was serious, he looked rather hurt.

'Cooper,' he said. 'Tommy Cooper.' And without smiling, he gathered up the receipt and bottle and walked out of the shop.

There were, of course, the usual gin drinkers, some quite well heeled. I recall one woman in particular who was taken by the spirit. She was the wife of a one-time local councillor and had taken a job as a domestic to pay for her little pleasure. As with the sticky British wine, she became exposed to the ravages of her tipple and was found unconscious in the lavatory of the hotel where she worked, still clutching her bottle of Gordon's Gin. She had been running an account with me for some time but, as usual, had failed the deadlines and had gone elsewhere for drink.

The last news I had of her was that she had been discovered by her husband standing in the window of their flat above the old greengrocer's shop in Clermont, totally naked and oblivious. She was taken to a psychiatric ward for treatment, but I think it was the end of the line for her.

There are so many victims of alcohol addiction, but to make the consumption of alcohol illegal is not a viable solution. Many of those who succumb are preordained in their genetic structure, while others continue unaffected by the compulsion to habitually over-imbibe.

George was the window cleaner for many of the shops along White Rock. Highly regarded as reliable and affordable, he would come round on Tuesday mornings to offer his services. He was usually cheerful, whistled while he worked, and was full of good advice.

In 1943, George was involved in the Sicily airborne landings. George recounted that he and most of the other gliders that had crashed into the sea the night of July 9th were casualties of the American towing aircraft when, running into enemy fire, the Americans released the British gliders too soon.

Over 200 English paratroopers landed in the sea and drowned. Taffy, a friend of his, panicked as he tried to scramble onto the wing of their sinking craft and somehow shot himself in the leg. George saw him slowly sink beneath the water. Many of them made it to shore, and the scene which greeted George and his comrades was something he could never forget.

He had reached a large cave or shelter in the rocks and found the remains of a shocking bloodbath. A local priest had tried to help some of the injured paratroopers to safety but, on being discovered by the Italian forces, were all systematically butchered with such violence that it was hard to identify the remains as human.

The memory haunted George until 1967, when his wife returned home from work to find the kitchen door locked from the inside. She could smell gas and called for help. George had sealed the room and, laying down in front of the gas cooker, he ended his nightmares forever.

Freddie Snow talked to me about going out on the road as a representative, and I think I could have done some good business for them, but nothing came of it. Meeting the rep that they did hire some years later, I was not surprised that the company fortunes had dwindled considerably. It wasn't his fault, but the company's strategy to sell inferior products to a discerning and selective clientele was a questionable business plan.

The new chairman replaced me as manager with his own protégé and asked me to sort out the cellars, check all the stocks and reserves, and make a list of everything that had gone astray. It took me three months, and at the end, I handed in my notice. I had literally run out of work.

For the record, there was something in the region of twenty thousand pounds worth of wine which was not accounted for, and this needed to be sorted out with London.

In the early nineties, Ellis, Son & Vidler underwent liquidation of its assets and ceased to exist.

35

In the autumn of 1971, I answered an ad in the local paper from the East Sussex Health Authority asking for applicants to work as auxiliaries in a geriatric unit in St Leonards-on-Sea. A lot of people did this type of work and some actually loved it. Bearing that in mind, I went for the interview.

What it didn't say in the paper was that the job was for a male auxiliary to work in a geriatric home for women. The interviewers looked me over and decided that I would do nicely and quickly showed me around the ward at Alexandra House.

My first introduction to the reality of frailty in old age was a rankled old lady sitting in a commode armchair. On seeing me enter the ward, she poked a gnarled, arthritic finger at me and gurgled.

I nearly fled in terror, but having been turned down as a paint sprayer because I was 'too qualified', I realised that there was absolutely no option but to carry on. Besides, I was to have the singular distinction of being the first male auxiliary to work on a female geriatric ward in the county.

I did a trial run on the daytime shift for the first week and became aware that it was not going to be an easy ride. It wasn't so much the patients who were the problem but the staff, several of whom had problems with me being the only male on the unit.

Questions were raised: 'What's he doing here? Is he a pervert? Is he homosexual and not bothered by working with women? Is he here for the drugs? He's so thin!'

A lot of the patients had suffered strokes and were bedridden. Some would wander in and out of reality, and some were there to die, but most were happy just to see a new face.

The job was actually for night work, 8pm to 8am, four nights one week and three the next. On my first night, the first introduction was to the sister on duty, followed by a meeting with my first corpse. The other auxiliary that night was sent off to take care of the rest of the patients while sister and I were to lay the poor dead woman out. Not only had I never seen a dead person before, but I had no idea what 'laying out ' entailed. I was to find out soon enough. I will say no more than that the process included wiping away stuff.

Her few possessions were placed in a bag and noted on a page. That done, the undertakers arrived. She was carried out in a large black hold-all, rather like a cricket bag but longer. Her bed was cleared and the next day, refilled with a new patient.

The nights could be quite interesting. The patients came from various social and economic backgrounds, and those that could speak had interesting stories to tell.

There was Mrs B who needed a crane to lift her. She was there because her family couldn't move her, and she was too weak to lift herself, but she was bright as a spark.

Mrs W, whose only word was 'alisaan', was locked in the nightmare of knowing what was going on but was incapable of communicating her needs. She was, for the most part, ignored and should have had some assistance just to break the monotony of sitting on a commode most of the day pleading 'alisaan' to any passerby. I did not understand the discomfort she must have felt and wish I had been more conscious of her misery.

Then there was Minnie, who had her toes cut off to stop her from running away, not by the medical staff, but by the Catholic sisters of the home in which she had been placed for having a relationship with a boy when she was young. Mentally, there was nothing wrong with her, but being only just past fifty, she had spent most of her adult life deprived of interaction with society and was now condemned to end her days in a geriatric unit.

Altogether, there were about twenty-three patients, only a few of whom were continent, and our job was basically to keep them dry, clean, and comfortable throughout the night. In the morning, a sister, another auxiliary, and I would give them tea, wash them, change their bedding, and return their false teeth. Some of those who had suffered a stroke and had lost the use of their hands had to have their teeth placed in their mouths, and that operation could become a little fraught.

On one occasion, a woman with the biggest set of teeth I had ever seen decided to use them on my thumb. She had the bite of a horse and wouldn't let go for several minutes, thrashing her head to inflict as much pain as she could. My thumb survived but carried distinctive teeth marks for a week or so. After that, I treated her with utmost caution and tried to avoid putting her teeth into her mouth.

Sometimes the other auxiliary would tap me on the shoulder and say, 'You put Mrs X's teeth in upside down', and sure enough, I had, but the patients never seemed to mind too much and were quite content to let me have another go.

Most of the nights, there was nothing to do except wait for the next round and listen for anyone calling out. I started to study the personalities of the other staff, and realised that years of night work can carry a toll on one's mental state. Some were more stalwart than others. Some went with the flow, but a few actually cracked.

There was one auxiliary who I usually worked with that was distinctly quirky. Everyone knew her as Chris, and though she was a top-quality worker, it took her a long time to come to terms with me. She had unbounded energy, looked about ten years younger than she really was, and was a do-it-yourself enthusiast.

She loved Plastic Padding and wore a lump of it on her fingernail for three weeks. She didn't believe I was teaching myself how to restore antique furniture, and by wearing the Plastic Padding, she confirmed that she knew how to do things. It was constantly on view which suggested that when it fell off, she must have glued it back on. I thought she was slightly mad.

Her style at work was amazing. She worked to a rhythm, one foot ahead of the other, and as she changed the bed linen, she could be seen rocking forwards and down, then up and back and down again, and before you knew it, the job was done. Tireless, she would move on to the next bed and then the next.

On her way home one morning, she spotted a new-looking lavatory pan in the rubble of some houses that were being demolished and decided that her bathroom needed to be renovated. One evening, she borrowed a child's pushchair and collected the lavatory pan, and a week later, she commented that it was working perfectly.

A year later, Alexandra House was shut down and Chris retired. She had, by that time, accepted me and became a decent friend, but the long nights of unemployment rapidly stole her youth, and her real age soon became apparent.

The Health Service was always understaffed, and being the least qualified at anything, I was sent from one hospital to another to fill in the shortage. After the closing of Alexandra House, I worked at the Eversfield Hospital in St. Leonards, still within the women's geriatric unit but more usually on loan to the male chest ward. This was a fairly tedious situation, often working with one staff nurse and a belligerent sister who could not accept that the world had changed.

Up to that time, there was no union operating at the hospital, and one of the nurses drew up an enrolment form for anyone who wished to join. This aggravated the sister so much that she threatened instant dismissal to anyone who signed, and they would never again work in the Health Service. I think that she believed she was more important than her position allowed.

She suffered from osteoporosis and was forever in plaster and of no use on the ward. During the night, she would install herself opposite me in the day room with her knitting and spend most of her time criticising me. The usual call was, 'Just look at you, you...you...vegetarian! Huh!' I thought that was rich coming from a person in her condition.

What I found strange was that she didn't seem to realise she was deteriorating quickly and never questioned why she had to use crutches, why her arm was in a plaster cast, or why she had to wear a neck brace. She was too clever to recognise that anything was wrong with her.

On the same shift was the regular staff nurse, who had been professionally trained as a chest nurse. She was all right most of the time, but had one irritating habit that nearly drove me mad. All the while she sat, her right foot would go backwards and forwards over and over, to the point where a large patch of the carpet had been worn down to the foundation. It was quite evident that she always sat in the same place.

Had the carpet been an ordinary one, it wouldn't have mattered so much. But it was a large and very rare Kazak prayer carpet dated 1878 which, in good condition, would have been worth many months' wages. Eventually, I could have bought it for next to nothing, but the problem of its use in a place where contagious TB was rife didn't appeal to me too much, and I wasn't prepared to take the risk.

I arrived at the chest ward one evening only to find the staff muttering under their breaths that we were going to have a 'night of it'.

'All they keep doing is asking for cups of tea and biscuits. They've been here all day. If they think this is a café...'

The problem was that a family of about seven was at the bedside of a terminally ill cancer patient, and they didn't want to miss the moment of his death. I thought it was rather sad, and I didn't fully understand the reasoning behind their insistence on being there in that precise moment. If the man woke up and saw all these faces peering at him, the shock would probably have hastened his end. The day staff had tried to reason with the family to go home but to no avail. They just had to be there at the end.

The patient was in a small room, and the relatives were milling around waiting for him to go. One of them, spotting me strolling down the corridor and mistaking me for somebody important (I assume it was the white coat) said, 'Doctor, will he still be here by the morning?'

Not knowing that the patient was dying, I took a quick glance at him and replied, 'Yes, he'll be here, don't worry,' and breezed off into the kitchen. The whole family packed up their books and bags and trotted off home. They returned promptly the next day at 8am, much to the annoyance of the day staff. The man died at around 10am.

When the family had gone after my assurances that evening, I thought my colleagues would have been relieved, but not so. I had impersonated a doctor, and that was an egregious crime. But as I pointed out to an irate sister, my badge clearly indicated that I was an auxiliary and not a doctor. Nonetheless, I was in everybody's bad books for the rest of the night.

Despite being a geriatric auxiliary, I spent most of my time on the various chest wards at the Eversfield. It always amazed me that patients were allowed to smoke in the wards, some of them with chronic bronchitis or emphysema and often right next to oxygen cylinders.

While helping the staff nurse hand out the various medicines and antibiotics to the patients, she asked me to give a suppository to one of the more breathless patients. These capsules, for some reason I can't quite fathom, were there to help with the breathing. How something shoved up one's bottom can help one breathe more easily was beyond me.

The patient, quite old and dingy from a life of chain-smoking, said, 'Be gentle, won't you, nurse?' Turning onto his stomach, he pushed his rear end up, out of the bed. I put on the requisite surgical gloves, and as I inserted the pill into his bottom, I held my breath and looked the other way, not liking what I was doing one bit.

'Oh! Oh, that's lovely, nurse. You're so gentle. I'll ask for you when I want another one,' he moaned, and turning, he held his hand out towards me.

He reminded me too much of Monty, and as I moved along the ward, he rolled another cigarette.

Shortly after that, I was to be sent off to the Bexhill Convalescent Home, but before I went, I had to pass that particular bed a couple of times, and each time I heard, 'Nurse, nurse! I need a suppository. Ow, nurse!' as I walked away, ignoring him.

One doesn't normally associate magic with hospital night work, but it can happen. It was about two in the morning in the East House annex to the chest ward that I became aware of movement in one of the rooms. I only had three patients to look after, and everything had been silent all night. An old man was wandering around in his room looking for a glass of water. I went in, gave him his glass, and helped him back to his bed. He asked me to sit with him for a short while as he drank the water. So we perched on the edge of his bed, side by side.

He told me that he was so happy, the happiest he had ever been. He had awoken from a dream in which he was being carried along by a school of whales and that it had been wonderful. 'They were so calm and gentle', he said.

He went on at some length to describe the intense beauty of the dream but, above all, to express his extreme happiness. When he had finished, he said he felt quite tired, so I helped him back into bed and said goodnight.

In the morning, he was dead.

I wrote in the night journal that he had woken up and that he was walking around in his room as I have described, but this did not fit with the previous journal entries, and I was asked to explain more fully the extent of my intervention. It appeared that he had not moved from his bed for three months, and as far as anyone knew, he was totally bedridden, unable to walk, and mostly unconscious over that period. What I had described was hard for them to accept, but seeing his joy was such a pleasure to have witnessed.

From magic to monstrous is a great distance, but between Hastings and St. Leonards, it was no more than a twenty-minute walk or five minutes in a taxi. At Eversfield, it was Sister R's mission, whose concern for the welfare of the geriatric staff was paramount, to finally expunge the evil that lurked in the male surgical ward at the East Sussex Hospital in Hastings.

As you may have guessed, I arrived at the East Sussex again on loan to help on the male surgical ward. The sister in charge was Sister M, and she had just returned to nursing after having had heart problems the previous year. It is possible that during surgery, the surgeon omitted to replace the organ. It is also possible that a vet was called in with a viper-heart replacement. Whatever drove this woman was in no way related to having a human heart.

I had been asked by one of the nursing officers to be easy on the woman due to her ill-health and not to expect her to be much help lifting any of the patients. Taking this on board, I initially accepted the situation.

Sister M laid down the rules of engagement from day one: no eating on the ward, and a break could only be taken between midnight and 2am. I was aware of this and didn't need to be told again, but okay.

We did the tour, handing out mainly painkillers to those who needed them and more serious drugs to those in acute pain. For one man who had gangrene in his toes, it was necessary to give him 20 mg of morphine and heroin (di-amorphine) which was to be delivered four times over a twenty-four-hour period, but only if he needed it. However, looking for a peaceful night, Sister M gave him a dose just in case.

I had understood that only qualified personnel were allowed to administer these drugs and that two had to be present, one to countersign the other in the dangerous drugs book. Neither state-enrolled nurses nor auxiliaries were allowed to take part in the process, so when sister M gave him the dose and told me to countersign her signature, I was rather surprised.

She disappeared from the ward for about an hour and, on returning, reiterated that I was not to eat anything until my break. She was just about to disappear once again when the man with gangrene groaned.

'I'm not having this!' she angrily declared and promptly went back to the drug cabinet. She measured out another three doses of the mixture and stood over the poor man until the overdose was consumed, then returned to her desk.

She signed for the drug another three times and handed me the book to countersign. I hesitated for a moment, knowing that this was not right, but I realised that should anything go wrong, by signing the book, it would prove that I had been a witness.

'Huh,' she said, 'that won't please the day staff.'

She returned briefly at midnight, and together, we quickly checked the patients. Everyone appeared to be asleep. She said that she was going to take her break and repeated that under no circumstances was I to eat anything in the ward or in the kitchen, and I must never leave the ward unattended. If I did any of these things, she would sack me immediately.

She returned at half past two and said that it was a pity, but it was now too late for me to have my break since the canteen closed at 2am. I was beginning to get a little cross as she turned around and disappeared once more.

I checked the patients at around 3am and found that a patient's bag of saline on the drip stand was empty, and not knowing how to change it, I asked for assistance from the auxiliary on the female ward next door. The bag was changed, and we chatted briefly about Sister M and the administration of the mixture. She told me that there were rumours of patients becoming ill during the night and sometimes dying for no particular reason when Sister M was on duty.

Sister M returned shortly after and, checking the beds, came to the stand with the new bag hanging.

'What's this?' she demanded to know, and I explained that it had been changed.

The words had barely left my mouth before she ripped the bag from its fixing and from the man's arm and threw the bag on the floor.

'I do this! How dare you change it without my permission. I'm going to have you sacked for this!' and on she raged.

I left the bag where it was and hoped that the patient would not suffer too much from this neglect.

At 6.30am, I started to make the patients tea and tried to prepare the wash bowls for those who needed them, but by 7.30 when the day staff came on duty, I was still way behind. Reluctantly, I was given a modicum of help, and having heard one complain that the washing up hadn't been done, I abandoned the ward to clear the tea things away.

Sister M returned at last, all sweetness and light at 7.45am and expressed her thanks for all I had done.

I couldn't believe it! I was absolutely incandescent with rage, and I let rip. The day staff in the kitchen were stunned as my language became more and more colourful. Sister M just stood there smiling in the doorway.

When I finished shouting and swearing at her, she turned and said, 'Thank you so much!' and left the room.

The day staff gave me a wide berth as if knowing from my outburst that since I had been deprived of food amongst other things, they might be on my menu. At 8.00am, I left the ward.

There was no transport available, and I finally arrived back at the Eversfield at 9am and related the story to a staff nurse. She immediately called Sister R.

'Nobody treats my staff like that and gets away with it! This is not going to happen again'. In turn, she reported the story to one of the nursing officers.

Immediately, a meeting was called with three nursing officers, and once more, I related the events. They checked the signatures and dosage in the dangerous drugs book at the East Sussex, and it was decided that Sister M had to go. I don't think that an investigation into her previous actions was conducted, perhaps a case of letting sleeping dogs lie. The best part of it was that Sister R put in for four hours extra pay for me to make up for my loss of time and poor treatment.

Hospital life was never dull, and sometimes the geriatric wards were a full-on circus and fairground. Only the bright lights and candy floss were missing. Acts like 'The Human Spring', 'Popeye', and 'The Amazingly Old Singing Lady' jumped into my mind for the inhumanity that life dealt out to some people.

Always totally saturated in urine no matter how often he was changed, and curled tightly in a fetal position, The Human Spring would suddenly uncoil with lightning speed whenever anybody went near him. The force generated was so great that he knocked one of the nurses unconscious with a single blow and recoiled into a fetal position in the blink of an eye.

Popeye was a one-legged sailor whose great pleasure was to call out to a passing nurse. Having attracted her attention, he would fling back the sheets, display his erection, and shout, 'See, I've got two legs now!'

Then there was the 102-year-old lady who was cared for in such a manner, it must have cost the health service thousands of pounds. She had a thermostatically controlled isolation room all to herself with a heated waterbed to lay on. She was rigidly fixed in one position with next to no flesh on her. She would lay completely naked on her side for twenty-four hours a day and utter a continual tuneless babble, which most of the staff decided was her singing.

'Isn't she wonderful', was a regular commentary. 'We must really look after her. She's so amazing!'

I never shared their enthusiasm. All I saw was a poor creature bereft of any human characteristics, who was being kept alive to see how long it could be done, as if it were a competition with a big prize at the end.

Epilogue

The last time I had the opportunity to go to the local tip, it filled me with amazement. It's astounding what people throw away, all sorts of stuff which others might be desperate to acquire There was a pretty little antique side table with a broken leg, the latter being safely tucked away in the drawer. There was a chest of drawers which needed a little attention, a winged armchair with a child's artwork on its seat.

There was one thing which caught my attention—a three-legged dog, a reject, a throwaway. Why was it there?

I asked the guy who ran the place, and he said, 'The owners were sick of the attention it was getting and decided it was time to throw it away.'

So there it sat patiently, with a sign next to it: 'Wanted! A Kind Heart'. It had been there for over two weeks, but nobody wanted a dog with three legs. It was different, not normal—a lost soul, perhaps.

While I sat there petting it, a sweet soul came by with a bowl of food for the animal. She watched him eat and then enquired, 'Has he no home?'

The reply was swift. 'If you take him, Missus, then surely he'll have one!'

I watched them go, the little throwaway hobbling along beside her, tethered close to the kind heart with a short length of rope.

And there you have it—a fanciful epilogue closing the door on the first three decades of my existence on this troubled earth.

Also by Barry Harden

Fiction
Ada & Eddie
Amanita Virosa: The Avenging Angel
The Demons of Mercantour
A Pantomime of Power

Nonfiction
*Throwaway: A Memoir of Growing Up in
Post-WW II London*

Short-Story Collection
*Strange Fruit: A Collection of Dark Allegories,
Fantasy, and Madness*

Poetry
Poems to Steal Your Dreams

About the Author

I am the author of four political thrillers, a collection of provocative short stories, and a book of poetry. Sociopolitical commentary is infused into my work, whether through fictional narratives, allegorical short stories or scathing satire that exposes the absurdities of human interaction with each other, animals, and the environment. I feel obligated to speak my truth as an individual and to reflect those truths as an author.

When not writing, I find solace in a glass (or two) of a well-aged Corbières while listening to Black jazz of the 20s and 30s. Born and raised in North Harrow, London, I now enjoy the peace and comfort of nature and wildlife and the company of my furry friends in my cat sanctuary. A change of scenery to the seashore on sunny days sparks creativity—without the distraction of my cats adding their input on the keyboard.

www.ingramcontent.com/pod-product-compliance
Lightning Source LLC
Chambersburg PA
CBHW030910120626
46554CB00001B/93